WEDDING ETIQUETTE

One of the many alternative arrangements
of part of a wedding breakfast table.

WEDDING ETIQUETTE

By

MARY WOODMAN

Revised by

GAVIN GIBBONS

The Engagement
The Wedding Arrangements
Legal Formalities
Duties of the Best Man
The Chief Bridesmaid
Wedding Toasts and Speeches
The Honeymoon and Afterwards
Marriage Symbols and Superstitions
The New Home
Anniversaries and Kindred Subjects

LONDON

W. FOULSHAM & CO., LTD.

NEW YORK TORONTO CAPE TOWN SYDNEY

W. FOULSHAM & CO. LTD.,
Yeovil Road, Slough, Berks., England.

ISBN 0-572-00005-7

MADE AND PRINTED IN GREAT BRITAIN BY
THE CAMELOT PRESS LTD, SOUTHAMPTON

PREFACE

TO THOSE ABOUT TO GET MARRIED, DO not spoil one of the most important occasions in your life by not knowing how a wedding should be arranged and the time-honoured customs connected with the celebration.

If you are about to play some part in a wedding celebration—whether as one of the two principal actors or in a lesser rôle—this book will pilot you successfully through its maze of intricacies. It begins by telling how the invitations should be issued, and explains every necessary step until the toasts are drunk at the reception, and the happy couple set out on their honeymoon. Not only are matters of etiquette fully dealt with, but the legal formalities are explained as well.

M.W.

MORALS FOR THE MARRIED

It takes two to make a quarrel.

Both husband and wife should never be angry at the same time.

Don't talk "at" one another before friends.

Don't belittle your wife's (or husband's) pastimes.

Don't squabble over the "in-law" relations. Take them for granted.

Don't forget his or her birthday.

Don't imagine that your point of view is the only one.

MAXIMS

Man's best possession is a sympathetic wife.

What is love? Two souls and one flesh.

It is best to love wisely, no doubt; but to love foolishly is better than not to be able to love at all.

All mankind loves a lover.

A flower cannot blossom without sunshine, and a man cannot live without love.

Love is master of the wisest. It is only fools who defy him.

Love is impulse, no doubt; but true love is impulse wisely directed.

CONTENTS

DIAGRAMS

WEDDING ETIQUETTE

CHAPTER I

COURTSHIPS AND ENGAGEMENTS

MEN and women will fall in love with each other as long as mankind exists. No-one can tell what it is that makes Jill seem to Jack the most wonderful person on Earth and that life without her would be unbearable. Neither is there anything tangible that makes Jill like Jack more than any other man she has met. The last people to be able to answer the question would be Jack and Jill themselves.

Falling in love is a state of wonder that brings romance and excitement into the most drab lives. It happens to most people, and for some it is the only real escape from dullness and drudgery that they have in their lives. For many others, more fortunate, falling in love marks the beginning of a new life, when everything is more wonderful and more exciting and problems are less burdensome as they are faced together. Many men look back upon their marriage as the time when their lives were changed for the better, their wives giving them that little bit of stimulus, which enabled them not only to do their jobs better, but to enjoy their lives more altogether. For nearly all of them it began when they first fell in love.

In the mid-twentieth century it is fashionable to have—or pretend to have—a somewhat negative outlook on life. It is the done thing, or "with it" to be completely materialistic and cynical in one's outlook, and many young people today face the world with a sneer or even a snarl, which is far removed from the excited sense of wonder that was held by their parents. Many young people today smile rarely, and cultivate an attitude of disillusion and discontent, which, underneath, they may not feel at all. People who are young have the herd instinct more than at any other age and what is being "with it" other than conforming with the rest of the age-group?

It is hardly surprising that this negative attitude has done a lot to destroy the romantic approach to love and marriage. The whole thing has been debased. The accent today is on physical sex at the cost of all else, and mutual respect has been cast to the winds. Much of the blame for this must be laid on the advertisements which appear on the mass media of television and the popular press. Girls are encouraged to use this lipstick or that scent or this girdle to make themselves "it"—physically irresistible to the other sex. Men are encouraged to buy hair cream, after-shave lotion, gay sporting clothes for just the same reason.

In this sophisticated and affluent age, children seem

to mature much earlier and the exciting adventure of childhood is made as short as possible. All the things that gave pleasure to the child in his or her early teens a generation ago are contemptuously dismissed as "kids' stuff" by those in the same age group today and the first love affairs begin at a frighteningly young age.

Furthermore, among many young people today there is a tendency to look on marriage as an unnecessary institution altogether, an outdated convention forced on young people by stuffy elders out of touch with reality. So many young people mistaking physical sex for love go from one casual relationship to another —and are always surprised that they do not find it satisfactory. Perhaps he had chosen the wrong girl, thinks the boy, while the girl wonders if she had been right in having an affair with this particular boy.

The thinking man or woman, whatever his or her background, will realize that there is something deeper in love than the mere physical side. Little wonder that the boy and girl having a casual relationship find it so unsatisfactory. There is nothing behind it, nothing permanent, nothing lasting, no affection, and most important of all, no respect. For a lifelong union respect and affection are more important than anything else. They will persist long after the physical attraction has faded. Darby will have respect and affection for Joan and Joan for Darby fifty years after their wedding day, while the physical attraction will have ceased many years before.

So Jack and Jill, if they are to make a success of their marriage must look beyond mere physical attraction. There must be that sense of wonder that makes everything in life seem more exciting. Indeed, this in itself is a good test. If, as a result of the friendship everything seems dull and tarnished, the association is not true love, but merely sex. If, on the contrary, everything seems wonderful, there is much more chance that the young couple are genuinely in love.

There are so many exciting little touches when people are in love such as the man's writing poems to the girl and sending her flowers, though the sending of Valentines has today often degenerated into something of a joke.

Even so, the path of true love is not smooth—to misquote the old proverb. The silent, secretive partner should be suspect. Men are more often to blame for this than women. But the man who finds the girl he loves silent and reticent about her past life should persist in finding all about it before they get married. A girl should not tie herself to a man whose past she knows nothing about. Even today, in the affluent society, there are still far too many marriages for the sake of money rather than true love.

There are many other reasons why young couples whether engaged or otherwise, sometimes realize that they are not really suited for each other once they have got to know each other better. Usually one of the parties reaches this conclusion before the other and there is almost invariably a certain amount of anguish on the part of the other. Indeed there can well be bitterness and anger, and the couple stoop to all sorts of unkind actions to vent their spleen on the person they once loved.

Usually after they agree to part the couple see no more of each other. The gifts are either returned or not returned, whatever they decide. But the best way—and it can happen—is for the two people to agree that they are not suited for each other and yet remain friends. In this case presents are rarely returned and when one or other of the partners get married their former love attends the wedding and becomes a lasting friend of the young couple. Unfortunately this ideal method of ending a romantic friendship and which causes no pain at all is not often achieved. Indeed it can be said that during the courtship period people rise to their highest —but can sink to their lowest in their whole lives.

But let us leave the unhappy couple who break off their engagement and turn to the lucky pair who are getting engaged. Very often it is the girl who chooses the man, though she does not let him see it. She skilfully emphasizes the things in her which attract him. Furthermore, as the proposal should come from the man and not from the woman, she will often use little stratagems to achieve the desired end, should the man be slow in proposing. A favourite trick is the hint that there is someone else in her life. Or perhaps she plays "hard-to-get."

On the other hand with many other couples the final issue has often been clear for a long time. But the man should not when he has proposed, immediately take the engagement ring from his pocket and give it to the girl. This suggests that he is taking her for granted which is hardly flattering to her. Conversely, he should not wait too long, but give her the ring within at least a fortnight. Some couples dispense with the engagement ring altogether; the man giving his fiancée a present instead.

Before making the purchase, both the man and his future bride should discuss the kind of ring that is preferred. As a rule, an engagement ring is studded with stones, and the choice of these depends very much on one's personal fancies. Often, the lady's birth-stone is chosen, but when there is no particular preference, it is always safe to decide on diamonds. Here is a list of birth-stones and their meanings, with the months for which they stand:

January	Garnets, for Constancy.
February	Amethysts, for Sincerity.
March	Bloodstones, for Courage.
April	Diamonds, for Purity

May	Emeralds, for Hope.
June	Agates, for Health.
July	Rubies, for Passion.
August	Sardonyx, for Conjugal Happiness.
September	Sapphires, for Repentance.
October	Opals, for Lovableness.
November	Topaz, for Cheerfulness.
December	Turquoises, for Unselfishness.

One of the most important and happy events that takes place after the engagement is the introduction of the future bride to her fiancé's parents. Just as happy is the day when the girl takes her future husband to meet her parents. They may live in the same town and have known each other already a long time, or they may live many miles apart. But the day of the dreaded formal interview of a young man with his future father-in-law is long past. Even the custom of asking permission has now gone—the younger generation are much too independent nowadays.

But if the tendency to independence of young people today has gone too far, there is another tendency that is very welcome. The grim "in-laws" of the past have largely disappeared. Very often—much more often than the musical hall comedian would have us suppose—a very real affection grows up between the husband and his wife's parents and the wife and her husband's parents. The two sets of parents often become very close friends indeed.

There is another aspect which is often forgotten. This book is written assuming that both the parents of the bride and the bridegroom are alive. But it often happens that this is not the case, especially if the couple marry in later years. The girl who has lost her father years before can almost find a second father in her father-in-law, and the same is true for the husband. Although the parent-in-law can never quite take the place of the parent who has died, he or she can often make up quite a lot for the earlier loss.

If the young couple have a duty to keep their parents informed of their intention before the marriage the two sets of parents have a duty to the young couple. Much unhappiness can be avoided if both make the effort to know and like each other. So the happiest marriages are those which start with not only mutual respect but good will and affection all round between the members of the two families.

CHAPTER II

THE WEDDING ARRANGEMENTS

"A MARRIAGE has been arranged——"

So runs the familiar notice in the advertisement columns of the society papers. The curt little notice is, in fact, the forerunner of much careful preparation and planning. It is very important, however, to remember that the public announcement is not a sufficient intimation in the case of near relatives and close friends. If they were to wake up one morning and read in the newspapers that their favourite niece, or nephew, or bosom friend, was on the point of getting married, there would be much heartburning. So, a little before the announcement is made public, the future bride and bridegroom decide who must be told the glad tidings in a more personal manner.

The two make a list of all their friends and relations who are to be told, then they sit down and write to each. Usually, the bride has by far the longer list, and if it is at all lengthy, she is helped by her mother. The letters merely state that "*Beryl is engaged to Captain Rupert Manwood, whom she has known ever since she was a small girl, and we are sure you will be glad to have this piece of news.*" A long letter is not called for; but do not say "*please excuse more now, as I have so many letters to write.*" This is because each recipient likes to feel that he or she is being specially favoured with the news and is not a mere unit in a big crowd of people.

Another point to remember is to post all the letters at the same time. If they are sent out a few one day and the remainder another, the late recipients may get to hear the news from those who were acquainted by the first batch, and this should be avoided at all costs.

The plans for the actual day must now be thought out. Is the wedding to take place in a church, chapel or before a registrar? Whichever form is selected, the bridegroom should lose no time in visiting the proper official and arranging the date and other details. The arrangements about the ceremony are then discussed at a meeting between the parents of the bride and those of the bridegroom. When the date of the wedding has been fixed, certain preliminary arrangements are put in hand.

An important point at this stage is the question of the bride's money. A generation or so ago, this went automatically to the husband, who, in his turn, was legally responsible for all expenses incurred by his wife. Nowadays, the husband retains his liability, but the woman is allowed full control of her own money.

It is usual for her father to arrange a marriage settlement, the principal object of which is to safeguard his daughter in case of any financial difficulties on the part of her husband. The girl's money is generally settled upon herself, without power to touch the capital. This means that the income comes to her regularly, yet she cannot impoverish herself by handing over the capital to her husband.

In most cases, a clause is inserted under which the income becomes payable to the husband during his lifetime, in case of his wife's death, while the capital will be disbursed at his death according to circumstances.

The invitations for the wedding should be issued well in advance of the ceremony—at least two weeks before, three being quite usual. The bride and her parents draw up one list and the bridegroom another of the people to be invited, but the bride's parents send out all the invitation cards. The list will be compiled, generally, by the aid of the "engagement list," but there are sure to be certain omissions and additions.

The invitation is always composed in the third person, never in the first. It should be printed for preference, and a copperplate will be used for the purpose. The following may serve as a specimen:

"*Mr. and Mrs. Edgar Burrows request the pleasure of . . . .'s company at the marriage of their daughter Beryl with Captain Rupert Manwood, at All Saints' Church, Mayfair, on Saturday, 27 April, at 1.45, and afterwards at a reception at 15 The Grove, Hyde Park.*"

On receiving this intimation, friends should reply within three days—the sooner the better—and the answer, like the invitation, must be drawn up in the third person. It is sent to the bride's parents.

As a result of the invitations, a number of wedding presents will be sure to flow in during the next few ensuing days. All are delivered to the bride, except those which are of a personal nature and intended solely for the bridegroom. Every one of these must be suitably acknowledged as quickly as possible. The bride replies to those people who have sent to her, but if the gifts are very numerous, someone—her sister or mother—can write a share of the replies.

Today there is a tendency for several friends to band together in groups and make one gift which is both valuable and highly useful.

When the presents arrive, they should be dealt with methodically, if there is to be a display of them on the day of the wedding, or if a list is to be made and exhibited in some conspicuous place at the reception. Unless this is done, it will be very easy to miss out one or more of them, and the donors may then take offence. The exhibit or the list will include the special gifts received by the bridegroom at his home.

In certain cases, friends will write and ask what present the young couple will prefer. This is a good plan, because it avoids useless duplication of gifts. The difficulty that arises on these occasions, however, is to know within reason how much the friend is prepared to spend. A way out of the embarrassment is to suggest articles that may cost little or much, according to their quality or number. For instance, the bride may ask for table silver, cutlery, household linen, or, if it is desirable to be more definite, an ink-stand for the study or a mirror for the hall. Each of these items may be procured at no great cost, or much may be expended on them, at will.

Very early on in the arrangements, it will be necessary to choose the best man and the bridesmaids, if there are to be any. These important people play a considerable part in the wedding ceremony when it is a full, public affair; but there is a tendency to do without them when the wedding is a quiet function to which nobody but intimate relatives are invited. Even on these occasions, a best man can give much useful assistance.

The best man should be unmarried, somebody with an aptitude for looking after details, and a man who will not be easily flustered. The cheery person who can rise to any occasion and get things done is welcome.

There are usually from four to six bridesmaids; but one, two, up to eight is perfectly reasonable. These, as a rule, are selected from the unmarried members of the two families; but often the bride's greatest school-friend is among the chosen. A chief bridesmaid is selected from the group. Usually, she is the bride's sister, should she have one still unmarried as a sister is often near at hand and can consult the bride a dozen times a day, if need be.

The dresses of the bridesmaids vary with the fashion of the moment, but it is the bride who decides on their colour and details. She has nothing to do with paying for them, unless she cares to treat them as personal presents. In appreciation of their services, it is the custom for the bridegroom to give each of the bridesmaids a suitable present; usually it takes the form of some small article of jewellery, which can be worn at the ceremony.

In some circles, the idea is favoured of dispensing with bridesmaids and having pages; but more often than not, when pages are present, they supplement the bridesmaids rather than take their place. The duty of the pages is to follow immediately behind the bride, attend to her train and perform similar offices. Their dress may be the clothes usually worn, to which is added little touches of gaiety by means of bows, favours, etc. But, more frequently, they are attired in a "period" costume of Tudor, Jacobean, Georgian, Directoire, or other outstanding style. The smaller the pages, the more attractive they generally are; but there is always the fear that very small ones may decide, at the last moment, to play the unconscious role of the *enfant terrible*. No presents should be given to these youngsters.

The bride should select the music to be performed at the church, choosing appropriate classical music; Mendelssohn's *Wedding March* is always popular although now perhaps considered too hackneyed. Many other pieces can be used instead.

At some ceremonies it is considered advisable to arrange with the church officials to have printed for distribution among the guests a pamphlet giving the wedding service only, as extracted from the Prayer Book. This is a good plan to adopt in the case of a large gathering, as the pamphlet can bear the names of the happy couple with date, name of church, and so on. It makes a good memento.

The selection of the bride's apparel will be a matter for considerable thought. Many brides wear a robe of the whitest silk; but just as often white is not worn and an afternoon dress or costume is considered in perfect good taste.

In past generations and even today in fashionable weddings the bridegroom will wear a black tail coat, a black waistcoat, a pair of pin-striped trousers, a silk hat, light spats, a tie with a quiet pattern on a black ground, and he should carry a pair of grey suede gloves. Nowadays the bridegroom usually wears a lounge suit and no hat.

When the eventful day arrives, there must be a tacit understanding that everybody takes up his or her position in good time. To be a moment late may very well throw the whole ceremony out of gear, and it would be a calamity for the bride, of all people, to be kept waiting.

A quarter of an hour before the appointed time, the visitors begin to arrive, and, a few minutes later, the bridesmaids await the arrival of the bride at the church door. A few young men friends have been asked, in advance, to show the guests into their seats, and as a rule, custom decrees that the bride's followers are conducted to the left-hand seats of the church and the bridegroom's friends to those on the right-hand.

While the assembly is gathering, the bridegroom enters with the best man and goes up to the chancel barrier, there to await his bride. She arrives last, usually in company with her father. Failing him, any close friend may serve instead, and it need not be a man. Taking his right arm she walks up the aisle, followed by the bridesmaids. Here she meets the bridegroom and takes up a position on his left, her father being on her left, but a trifle in the rear. The best man stands on the right of the bridegroom, and like the father, he too falls a trifle in the rear.

The ceremony then commences, and just before the all-important moment is reached, the bride hands her bouquet, if she is carrying one, to the chief bridesmaid, and removes her glove from the left hand, if she is wearing gloves. At the proper time, the clergyman gives the ring to the bridegroom—or the best man may do this—and he slips it on to the third finger of his bride's left hand.

At the conclusion of the ceremony, the happy couple, escorted by their nearest friends and relatives pass into the vestry to sign the register, and receive the "marriage lines," which is the property of the bride. The bride signs her maiden name in the register, and takes the *left* arm of the bridegroom, as they leave the church for home, using the first car, followed by the bride's mother and the bridegroom's father; then the bridegroom's mother and the bride's father; next the bridesmaids, while after that the order is determined by age and relationship; but the best man is usually last of all.

It will be noted that throughout the whole of the time, from the moment the first arrangements are made to the time when the ceremony is over, the bride's mother plays practically no official part at all. Nevertheless, her duties are by no means light, seeing that she must advise her daughter on so many matters and help her in so many ways. In the case of a motherless bride, a married sister or a favoured aunt may well perform these duties.

Once the whole party has reached home, or the hall appointed for the reception, the bride's parents welcome the guests, who say complimentary things to the newly married couple, and inspect the presents, if they are spread out.

The festivities may take the form of a reception, when light refreshments are placed on a buffet and handed round in the drawing-room. These consist of tea, wines, claret cup, sandwiches, fancy cakes, etc.

If a breakfast or luncheon is provided, the bride and bridegroom take their places at the head of the table, the wife on the husband's left. On her left sits her father and then her mother-in-law. On the bridegroom's right sits his mother-in-law and then his father.

Although spoken of as a "breakfast," this repast should consist of (1) soup, (2) fish, (3) entrées, (4) roast joints, poultry, (5) sweets, (6) cheese, (7) dessert, followed by coffee.

If the wedding takes place close to the limit of six o'clock, a tea is sometimes provided instead of a breakfast, though we think that a reception would prove more suitable. The tea should be a "high tea," at which the guests sit round the table in the dining-room.

The wedding cake is cut by the bride, with the assistance of her husband. Everybody present must partake of it. The most appropriate moment will depend upon the nature of the gathering.

Whilst speaking of the wedding cake, we may refer to the custom of sending small sections of it to absent friends and well-wishers. This is not done until some days after the ceremony, and, sometimes, not before the bride and bridegroom return from their honeymoon. The usual plan is to obtain a number of small boxes, which stationers sell for the purpose, to put a slice of cake in each, not forgetting a fragment of the icing, and to include a specially printed card.

Cards of various shapes and patterns are to be had. As well as the names of the couple they give the place and time of the wedding. The bride's maiden name appears in a corner struck through with an arrow.

It is well to enclose the box in a stiff envelope, somewhat larger than the box itself. If this is done, there is less chance of the package going astray in transit.

When the meal in whatever form it takes, is about half-way through, the time for the first toast is at hand. No matter how informal the gathering, there should be at least the toast which proposes "Health and happiness to the bride and bridegroom." Usually the bride's father stands and proposes it. The bridegroom then responds briefly and generally ends by adding a toast to the health of the bridesmaids. The best man follows by replying for the bridesmaids, and the bridegroom's father usually adds a few words. The bride may elect to say something quite short and brief; but, as a rule, she contents herself by smiling an approval of her husband's words.

None of the speeches should be long; they should all be of a brief character, and if witty remarks can be made without creating offence, so much the better. There is no need for formal speeches, while to read one or to use notes would be supremely out of place. An avowal of one's lack of oratorical capabilities will usually get a bad speaker over his initial troubles, and after that the rest should be easy. The bridegroom, usually, tells the gathering that he is the most fortunate of men, he comments on the general good looks of the bridesmaids, and he never fails to express his wonder at the best man's single state, when there are so many attractive and eligible young ladies awaiting a similar fate to that of his wife.

The time for the guests to depart varies, but they should all remain until the bride and bridegroom have said "good-bye" and set out for their honeymoon.

The bride's parents should prepare a short notice of the day's events, which should be sent to the editor of the local newspaper; a reporter *may* have been present, but it is not wise to rely on reporters.

When a wedding takes place in a country district, some sort of accommodation must be found for the guests who come from a distance. The bride's father should make the necessary arrangements, seeing that he has more facility than the guests to do so. Neighbours can often offer a certain amount of accommodation; rooms can also be engaged at the local hotel, while his own house will be crowded to its utmost limits.

In the unfortunate event of a family bereavement, there is no other course than to postpone the wedding.

This will necessitate notices being sent to all who have signified their intention of attending the wedding. Such notices will merely state the facts, and the wording should be framed in the third person.

CHAPTER III

HOW TO GET MARRIED

In the case of a second or subsequent marriage, the general details supplied in this chapter should be studied in conjunction with Chapter VII.

THERE are several ways of taking the all-important step of getting married. This chapter deals with them mainly from the legal aspect. With the exception of the Jewish ceremony, and the Special Licence, which costs £25 or more and is not easily obtained, no wedding can take place later than 6 p.m.

BY BANNS

This is probably the method preferred by most people today. Should it be the form chosen, the first thing is to call upon the vicar or rector of the church in which the marriage is to be solemnized, and to ask him to allow the ceremony to take place in his church. If he is to officiate, that matter should also be discussed, and, of course, if a clergyman who is a friend of the family is preferred, permission must be sought at the same time for him to do so. When these preliminaries have been arranged, and the clergyman has satisfied himself that the parties are of full age, or that they have the consent of their parents, he will proceed to publish the banns.

The banns are published by being read aloud in church on three Sundays preceding the ceremony. The rubric provides that the proper place for the announcement is immediately after the second lesson in the service.

Here it is important to note that when the two parties do not live in the same parish, as is frequently the case, the banns must be read in duplicate, (a) in the parish of the man and (b) in that of the woman. In such cases, it is necessary to obtain a certificate from one clergyman (whose church is not being used) to give to the other clergyman in whose church the ceremony is to take place. This certificate states that the banns have been called legally, and without it, no other clergyman can proceed with the wedding service.

If neither of the two live in the parish in which it is desired that the ceremony should take place, the man usually obtains a room in the parish and resides there during the week-ends. In this way, he fulfils the residence qualification of fifteen days. It is not essential that he should live in the strange parish on every day of this period, but he must sleep there on at least one night in each week.

When the banns have been published properly, the

wedding may be solemnized on any day within the three following months.

Since the system of marriage by banns has been devised to give publicity to the forthcoming wedding, it is fraudulent to substitute misleading names for the proper ones; indeed, the marriage may then be null and void. If only one of the parties gives the correct name, the marriage is not affected legally, but the defaulter might be imprisoned for perjury. When a person is generally known by a name which is not his or her legal name, the banns should give the one more generally known, or include both, as for instance "Agnes (Dolly) Jones."

By Licence

There are two different ways of being married by licence. The first is generally spoken of as "the common or ordinary licence," which is granted by the Surrogates for the Archbishop or Bishop of the diocese, when the ceremony may take place in any church properly licensed for such purposes. The second is termed "by special licence." This is granted by the Archbishop of Canterbury.

Ordinary Licences may be sought at the following addresses:

(a) The Faculty Office, 1 The Sanctuary, Westminster, London, S.W.1. A licence obtained here may be used in any church, licensed for weddings, throughout England and Wales.

(b) The Bishop's Registry Office, situated in every cathedral town. The office of the Bishop of London is to be found at 1 Dean's Court, Doctors' Commons, E.C.4. A licence obtained at one of these offices may be used only in the diocese in which it is issued.

In applying at any of the above offices, it is necessary that one of the parties to the marriage must appear in person. In other words, it is quite useless to send a friend or the best man, even though he may be empowered in writing to act for the parties.

The person making the application is required to sign a declaration, on oath, stating (a) that there is no legal reason why the marriage cannot properly take place, and (b) that either the man or the woman, or both, have had their ordinary place of abode for fifteen days at least, prior to the application, within the area served by the church that is to be used for the ceremony. This is known as the residence qualification.

The advantages of being married by ordinary licence are (a) banns are unnecessary, (b) the marriage can take place as soon as the licence is issued, and (c) the fees are reasonable. It is certainly a method which should be given full consideration, particularly when, for some reason, the banns have not been published properly.

The cost of getting married in a church is as follows:

(*a*) By Banns:	£ p.
Publication of Banns	0.75 to the Minister
	0.30 to the Clerk
Marriage Fee after Banns (where organ not used).	2.00 to the Minister
	1.00 to the Clerk
	1.00 to the P.C.C.
Certificate of Banns	0.50 to the Minister
	0.20 to the Clerk
Marriage Fee after Banns (where organ used)*	4.00 to the Minister
	2.00 to the Clerk
	2.00 to the P.C.C.
(*b*) By Licence:	£ p.
Ordinary Licence	4.50
Marriage Fee after Licence	2.00 to the Minister
	1.00 to the Clerk
	1.00 to the P.C.C.
Subsequent certificate of Marriage	0.40

This has nothing to do with the wedding, where there is no charge for the Marriage Certificate.

* This is not inclusive of the organist's fee which is arranged between the Minister and the parties concerned.

(Note: Stamp duty on Ordinary Licences has been abolished.)

Special Licences are only issued by the Archbishop of Canterbury at the Faculty Office, 1 The Sanctuary, Westminster, S.W.1. Before granting such a licence, His Grace must be satisfied that there is some special and urgent reason why the more ordinary methods of solemnizing the marriage are unsuitable in the applicant's case.

When granted, a special licence permits the wedding to take place on any date in any church, properly licensed. Thus there are neither restrictions as to the residence of the parties, nor as to the time.

The cost of a Special Licence is £25. Stamp duty has been abolished.

Before a Registrar

When, for one of various reasons, the bride does not wish to be married at a church, the ceremony can take place in the office of a registrar. In this case, the first step is to call on the local Superintendent Registrar, the Registrar of Marriages, or the deputy of these officials, who will arrange the function in one of these two ways:

By Certificate.—The official, in this case, will provide a form to be filled in, which requires the names of the parties, their residences, and their ages. It also necessitates mention of the building at which the wedding is to take place, and concludes with a declaration, to be signed, which states that there is no legal objection to the marriage, and that the consent of the parents is forthcoming in the case of minors. If any false information is given on this form, severe penalties are provided.

The residence qualifications required for a certificate are (a) both the man and woman must have lived, for seven days prior to the visit, in the area controlled by the registrar. One of the two only need then appear and make the declaration; (b) when the man and woman live in areas controlled by different registrars, they must each make the declaration before their own district registrar, and they must both have lived in their respective areas for seven days prior to the visit.

On being satisfied with the information supplied to him, the Superintendent Registrar will make the necessary entry in his notice book, and twenty-one days later, he will issue the certificate for the marriage. The ceremony can then take place at any time within the three months following the entry in the notice book, NOT WITHIN THREE MONTHS FOLLOWING THE ISSUE OF THE CERTIFICATE.

By Licence.—In this case, a similar declaration must be made and signed, as mentioned for a marriage by certificate, but the residence qualifications are different. For a licence, only one of the parties need visit the registrar to make the arrangements, even though the two live in different registration areas; but the one who elects to appear must have lived in the area for fifteen days prior to the visit.

On being satisfied with the information supplied to him, the Superintendent Registrar will make the necessary entry in his notice book, and one clear day after he will issue the licence for the marriage; but Sundays, Christmas Day and Good Friday are not counted. The Licence is valid for three months.

Charges.—The legal charges entailed by a marriage at a registrar's office are as follows:

(*a*) By Certificate	£ p.
Entering Notice of Marriage	1.00
Certificate for Marriage	0.50
Marriage Attendance Fee	1.50
	£3.00

(Note: If the parties live in different districts, notice has to be entered and a certificate issued by each Registrar, thus increasing the total charges by £1.00)

(*b*) By Licence	£ p.
Entering Notice of Marriage	1.00
Certificate and Licence for Marriage	5.00
Marriage Attendance Fee	1.50
	£7.50

(Note: Stamp Duty on marriage licences has been abolished.)

The cost of a certified copy of the entry of Marriage—the equivalent of the Certificate of Marriage issued after a marriage in Church—is 50p for marriage by certificate or licence.

Documents.—On proceeding to the ceremony, the following documents must be taken with the parties to be married and handed to the officiating registrar. Probably, these will be in safest keeping if entrusted to the best man beforehand.

(a) For a marriage by certificate, the certificate issued by the registrar when both parties live in the same area; or the certificates issued by the two registrars when the parties live in different areas.

(b) For a marriage by licence, the certificate issued by the registrar in whose area the notice was given.

Two persons must be present at the wedding, who

will be required to sign their names as witnesses to the ceremony. They can be total strangers to each other, and to the couple about to be married.

Nonconformist Weddings

People who are Nonconformists may be married in a chapel. The requirements are similar to those mentioned above for marriage before a registrar, and, indeed, the Registrar of Marriages must be present to perform the duties, unless the following paragraph applies.

The Marriage Act of 1898 makes his presence unnecessary when the chapel has been registered and has also adopted the provisions of the 1898 Act. By this Act, the minister or other authorized person may perform the duties usually performed by a registrar. This only applies to England and Wales.

When the ceremony is conducted in this way, each of the contracting parties must make the following declaration at some point in the wedding service:

"I do solemnly declare that I know not of any lawful impediment why I, (so and so), may not be joined in matrimony to (so and so)."

Then, having said this, they must turn to each other and say:

"I call upon these persons here present to witness that I, (so and so), do take thee, (so and so), to be my lawful wedded husband (or wife)."

Jewish Weddings

When Jewish people marry, they are required to give notice to the registrar, as set out earlier, but the marriage may be solemnized in a synagogue or private house, and need not take place at the registrar's office. When a synagogue or house is used, the secretary of the synagogue to which the man belongs must take down the necessary official particulars. The only other legal point to note is that a Jewish wedding may take place at any hour of the day, and not necessarily before 6 p.m. as is required for all other people.

The ceremony, when held in a synagogue, varies a good deal in the form it takes. At the United Synagogue, the service is of a very ancient and interesting nature. The bride and bridegroom sit under a canopy, which is intended to recall the time when the Israelites were forced to live in tents. Behind them are arrayed their relations and friends. In front is the officiating rabbi, who delivers a short address to the two young people.

Then the bridegroom turns to his future wife and says, "Behold, thou art consecrated unto me by this ring, according to the law of Moses and Israel." Then he places a ring on her hand.

The next step is the reading and signing of the Hebrew marriage contract.

The official, addressing both the man and the woman, says: "You, ... , and you, ... , are about to be wedded according to the law of Moses and of Israel." Then, turning to the man, he asks: "Will you, . . . , take this woman, . . . , to be your wedded wife? Will you be a true and faithful husband unto her? Will you protect and support her? Will you love, honour and cherish her?"

The bridegroom answers, "I will."

The official then addresses the woman. "Will you, . . . , take this man, ... , to be your wedded husband? Will you be a true and faithful wife to him? Will you love, honour and cherish him?"

The bride's reply is, "I will."

Following these vows, the Seven Benedictions are recited and the two people partake twice of wine from the same vessel; then the husband dashes the glass on the ground and smashes it. The drinking of wine, twice, is done to remind the couple that they are required to share each other's pleasures and halve each other's troubles. The smashing of the glass symbolizes the weakness of marriage when robbed of love.

Before the ceremony is concluded, the following covenant has to be signed properly:

"On the . . . day of the week, the . . . day of the month of . . . in the year . . . , corresponding to the . . . of . . . , the Holy covenant of marriage was entered into, in . . . , between the bridegroom, . . . , and his bride, . . .

"The said bridegroom made the following declaration to his bride: 'Be thou my wife according to the Law of Moses and of Israel. I faithfully promise that I will be a true husband unto thee. I will honour and cherish thee; I will work for thee; I will protect and support thee; and will provide all that is necessary for thy due sustenance, even as it beseemeth a Jewish husband to do. I also take upon myself all such further obligations for thy maintenance during thy lifetime as are prescribed by our religious statutes.'

"And the said bride plighted her troth unto him, in affection and with sincerity, and has thus taken upon herself the fulfilment of all the duties incumbent upon a Jewish wife.

"This covenant of marriage was duly executed and witnessed this day according to the usage of Israel."

Roman Catholic Weddings

The marriage service in the Roman Catholic Church is very similar to that in Protestant churches, but there is no mention of "obedience", and the bridegroom holds the right hand of his bride and says:

"I, . . . , take thee, . . . , to be my wedded wife, to have and to hold, from this day forward, for better, for worse, for richer, for poorer, in sickness and in health, till death us do part, if Holy Church will it permit; and thereat I plight thee my troth."

The ring, however, plays a much more important part in the ceremony than it does in the Church of

England service. The priest having said to the pair, "I join you together in marriage, in the name of the Father and of the Son and of the Holy Ghost, Amen," he sprinkles the two with holy water, and the bridegroom places the ring on the book, together with pieces of gold and silver. After it has been blessed, the bridegroom presents the gold and silver to the bride, saying:

"With this ring, I thee wed; this gold and silver I give thee; with my body I thee worship; and with all my worldly goods I thee endow."

Following this, the bridegroom places the ring on the thumb of the bride's left hand and says: "In the name of the Father." Quickly slipping it on to the index finger, he continues: "And of the Son." Then transferring it to the next finger he proceeds: "And of the Holy Ghost." Finally, putting it on the third finger, he utters the word, "Amen." The ceremony is then concluded with prayers, one of which is for the bride. It is worded as follows:

"Let the yoke of love and of peace be upon her. Let her be lovely in the eyes of her husband, even as was Rachel; let her be wise, as was Rebecca; let her live long and be faithful, as was Sarah. Let the author of mischief have no part in any of her doings."

Quaker Weddings

When a wedding is to take place in a Meeting House of the Society of Friends, the first essential is that a registrar should be present to legalize the marriage.

The usual custom is for the bride and bridegroom to sit surrounded by their relations and friends, and then for the two to stand at a prearranged moment. Holding hands, the man makes the following declaration.

"Friends, I take this, my friend, . . . , to be my wife, promising, through Divine assistance, to be unto her a loving and faithful husband until it shall please the Lord by death to separate us."

The bride makes a similar declaration, altered to suit her needs.

Following this, a certificate is drawn up, stating that the couple made the necessary declaration, that they fulfilled the legal obligations and were duly married.

No ring appears at all in the ceremony, but for the sake of expediency, the bridegroom usually presents one to his wife as soon as the religious and legal matters are concluded.

It should be added that notice must be given prior to the ceremony, to the proper quarters, in the manner set out for Nonconformist weddings. In addition, a Quaker wedding cannot take place until the Society has "liberated" the two young people—that is, until the Society has given them a certificate stating that they are considered fit and proper persons to marry. This liberating form is worded as follows:

"AB and CD, being desirous of taking each other in

marriage, and having complied with the regulations of the religious Society of Friends in relation thereto, the needful documents having been produced to this meeting, and the necessary public notice having also been given, the parties are left at liberty to solemnize their intended marriage."

Naval Weddings

By the Naval Marriages Act of 1908, it was recognized that members of the Royal Navy have difficulty at times in fulfilling the residential qualifications mentioned in various places in the preceding pages. Accordingly, the Act permits any officer, seaman or marine, aboard ship, to have the banns published by his chaplain, or commanding officer, in the manner prescribed under the sub-heading *Banns* on pages 32-34. Or, if the wedding is to be solemnized in a registrar's office or duly registered Nonconformist chapel, the commanding officer may take the particulars as is usually done by the Registrar, and issue the necessary certificate on the expiry of a period of twenty-one days.

Note that marriage by licence is not affected by this Act, also that the prospective wife must arrange matters on shore in the manner already described.

Forbidden Marriages

Marriages are forbidden between people of certain

close relationship. Under the heading of *A Table of Kindred and Affinity wherein whosoever are related are forbidden in Scripture and our laws to marry together*, the Prayer Book gives the following information:

(a) A man may not marry his grandmother, grandfather's wife, wife's grandmother, father's sister, mother's sister, father's brother's wife,* mother's brother's wife,* wife's father's sister,* wife's mother's sister,* mother, step-mother, wife's mother, daughter, wife's daughter, son's wife, sister, wife's sister,* brother's wife,* son's daughter, daughter's daughter, son's son's wife, daughter's son's wife, wife's son's daughter, wife's daughter's daughter, brother's daughter, sister's daughter, brother's son's wife,* sister's son's wife,* wife's brother's daughter,* and wife's sister's daughter.*

(b) A woman may not marry with her grandfather, grandmother's husband, husband's grandfather, father's brother, mother's brother, father's sister's husband,* mother's sister's husband,* husband's father's brother,* husband's mother's brother,* father, step-father, husband's father, son, husband's son, daughter's husband, brother, husband's brother,* sister's husband,* son's son, daughter's son, son's daughter's husband, daughter's daughter's husband, husband's son's son, husband's daughter's son, brother's son, sister's son, brother's daughter's husband,*

* See page 48.

sister's daughter's husband, husband's brother's son, and husband's sister's son.

Most of the relationships set out above are so obviously barred as to be without interest. Occasionally, however, cases arise when people wishing to marry come within one of the affinities set out in the Prayer Book. Usually, it is a husband who desires to marry his wife's sister, or a wife, her husband's brother. So insistent have been these particular desires that Parliament gave the question very full consideration in 1907 and again in 1921. After much deliberation, the Act of 1907 made it legal for a man to marry his deceased wife's sister, or deceased brother's wife; while the Act of 1921 gave similar consent to a woman marrying her deceased husband's brother or her deceased sister's husband. A further Act, passed in 1931, made legal provision for the marriage of persons with their nephew or niece by marriage.

It is, however, still illegal for a man to marry his divorced wife's sister, during his wife's lifetime, or similarly, for a woman to marry her divorced husband's brother, during her husband's lifetime. The same prohibition applies to the relationships specified in the Act of 1931, if the previous marriage has been dissolved by divorce.

Miscellaneous Information

The following miscellaneous paragraphs are important, seeing that they refer, in the main, to what has been said already.

(a) Marriages must be solemnized between the hours of 8 a.m. and 6 p.m. The only exceptions are set out at the head of this chapter.

(b) The doors of a building must be left open while a marriage ceremony is proceeding.

(c) In theory, a wedding cannot be private.

(d) When a divorced person desires to be married again, he or she must produce the decree of divorce.

(e) A marriage that has taken place in a registrar's office may be solemnized in a church, at any later date, but the registrar's certificate must be handed to the clergyman, and the ceremony will not be recorded afresh as a marriage.

(f) People under 21 may not marry, except with the consent of the parents of both parties, or the approval of a magistrate. If the parents of either or both are dead, then whoever acts as guardian must give the necessary consent—see the Guardianship of Infants Act, 1925. Under an Act of Parliament passed in 1929, no person, whether male or female, may marry legally under the age of 16, even with the consent of parents or guardians.

(g) A clergyman is not obliged to conduct the marriage service if one or both of the parties have been divorced, even if the divorce decree has been granted to, and not against, such person; but though he may refuse to officiate personally, he cannot withhold permission for someone else in Holy Orders to perform the ceremony in his church.

(h) Neither party to a divorce may re-marry until the "decree absolute" has been granted. This decree has to be applied for by the successful petitioner six weeks after the issue of the "decree nisi."

It is a general misconception that the Respondent may marry again immediately after a "decree nisi" has been proclaimed.

Up to the present, all that has been laid down applies to England and Wales, and, in part, to Northern Ireland. But various difficulties of a confusing nature are liable to arise when the parties (or one of them) are connected with countries outside the above areas.

When One of the Parties Lives in Scotland

the procedure has to be varied slightly. The person living in England or Wales acts exactly as already stated according to the form of marriage desired. The party living in Scotland must also give notice of marriage in accordance with the provisions described under the heading, *Marriages in Scotland.*

Since the Marriage Act, passed in 1939, notices issued in England and Wales are valid in Scotland, and vice versa, provided only one of the parties resides in Scotland. Note, however, that marriage by licence in a registrar's office in England or Wales is not possible in these cases.

When One of the Parties Lives in Northern Ireland

the procedure is similar to that set out in the two preceding paragraphs except that, in Northern Ireland, notice is given to the District Registrar of Marriages, while the residence qualification is seven days instead of fifteen days, as in Scotland.

Marriages in Scotland

Marriage in Scotland may only take place provided one or both of the parties have been resident there for fifteen days. It is important to remember that, under Scots law, the legal day is reckoned from midnight to midnight. In the case of a person who is not permanently domiciled in Scotland, the day of arrival and the day of departure do not count as part of the legal period of residence.

"Irregular marriages" have for long been a feature of Scottish matrimonial law without any parallel in England, and in the past many romantic adventures reached their climax at the blacksmith's anvil at Gretna Green. Under recent legislation, however, irregular marriages by declaration in the presence of two witnesses and by other quaint methods are no longer valid under law.

(a) Marriages may be solemnized before a minister of one denomination or another in the presence of two witnesses aged sixteen years or over.

It is required that one of the contracting parties must have been resident in Scotland for fifteen days immediately prior to giving notice of marriage while the wedding must have been publicly proclaimed by banns or by "notice."

By law, the banns must be read in church on three consecutive Sundays; but common consent has long deemed one Sunday sufficient. The necessary certificate is then issued at a fee of 2*s.* 6*d.*, and it is available for three months.

(b) Marriage before a Registrar is now governed by the Marriage Act, 1939.

When notice of marriage is given to a registrar, he records particulars in his register on payment of a fee of 1*s.* 6*d.* and the details of such entries are then posted up on the outer wall of his office. If both parties to the marriage live in the same parish or district, one notice, given jointly, is sufficient: but if the man and woman reside in different districts, each must give notice individually to their respective registrars, and pay the fees for the entries of notice and certificates of due publication independently.

After the expiry of seven days, application must be

made for a certificate of due publication which the registrar will issue at a fee of 1*s.* provided nobody has lodged any objection which is likely to debar the marriage. Each party must obtain separate certificates if residing in different districts. The wedding may then take place at any time within three months.

On production of a registrar's certificate or certificates of due publication in respect of both parties, the couple, in the presence of the registrar and of two witnesses of the age of sixteen years or upwards, declare that they know of no legal impediment to their marriage and that they accept each other as husband and wife. The registrar then issues a marriage certificate, in the form required by the Act, which is signed by the parties to the marriage, the registrar and the two witnesses. The fee payable to the registrar is 5*s.* The marriage is valid unless there is a legal impediment.

The fee for a certificate of marriage contracted before either a Minister or a Registrar is 2*s.* if ordered at the time of Registration or 3*s.* if requisitioned at a later date.

If a party is ill or some other unforeseen or exceptional circumstances prevent one of the parties from giving the required notice or arranging for the publication of banns within the time required, a joint application may be made to the sheriff for a licence. If a sheriff's licence is obtained, the marriage must take place within ten days of it being granted.

(c) If a Quaker wedding is desired and either one or both parties is a member of or an attender associated with the society of Friends, notice of marriage must be given to the local Registrar in the manner already described, and a certificate of due publication be obtained before the Quaker ceremony may take place.

(d) Before a Jewish ceremony may be performed in Scotland, the same procedure as for Quakers applies except that both parties must be members of the Jewish faith.

(e) The Naval Marriages Act of 1908 applies to Scotland in exactly the same way as described previously for England and Wales.

(f) Parties divorced under Scottish law may marry again immediately, as the Scottish decree is absolute from the time that a divorce is granted.

Marriages of British Subjects in Foreign Countries

Marriages of British subjects in foreign countries are recognized under the Foreign Marriage Act of 1892. They are as valid as marriages solemnized in England, provided that they are celebrated either in accordance with local law or in the presence of British diplomatic or consular agents who have been empowered to act as "marriage officers." It is immaterial whether or not the marriage takes place in a Christian country. Under

British law a heathen ceremony is equally valid, so long as it is in accordance with the law of the country in which the ceremony takes place, and provided the marriage is monogamous—that is, provided it prevents the man who enters it marrying any other woman while his wife is still alive and not divorced from him.

A marriage may be solemnized on board one of Her Majesty's ships at a foreign station provided the commanding officer holds a warrant of a secretary of state to act as marriage officer. At sea marriages on British naval and merchant vessels are valid provided they are performed by an episcopally ordained minister.

The procedure for marriage of serving members of the Royal Navy has been described on page 46. Marriages performed by chaplains in units of the Army and the R.A.F. are, of course, valid irrespective of where the units happen to be stationed.

Marriages of British and Foreign Subjects

At one time a foreign woman marrying a British subject automatically gained British nationality, while a British woman marrying a foreigner automatically lost it. This state of affairs has been completely changed as from January, 1949.

A woman of non-British nationality marrying a British subject now has to apply to the Secretary of State if she wishes to acquire British nationality.

A British woman marrying a foreigner is now

entitled to retain her British nationality after marriage if she so desires.

Nationality laws vary considerably from one country to another, and if a British woman marrying a foreigner intends to live in her husband's country, she ought to acquaint herself in advance with its laws. Some countries, she will find, confer their nationality on her automatically, but others require her to qualify for naturalization like any other alien.

A Marriage is Void

(1) When the contracting parties come within the prohibited relationships as set out in the Prayer Book—except in so far as these prohibitions have been waived by Acts of Parliament (see page 48).

(2) When one, or both of the parties, has committed bigamy, by going through the marriage ceremony, a legal wife (or husband) having been alive at the time.

(3) When one or both the parties is insane at the actual time of the marriage, or when one or both the parties has already been certified as insane but has not been considered to have regained his or her mental balance. Note that the marriage is binding if insanity can only be proved to have become evident after marriage.

(4) When both the parties are married under fictitious names, the marriage may be void.

Before concluding, a word of warning should be

given to the British woman who contemplates marriage with a man whose religion permits him to marry several wives, or who hails from a country that allows him to throw off the marriage yoke with impunity. Such a union may prove happy, but far too many do not, and, at the very least, the step should not be taken until friendly as well as legal advice has been considered.

CHAPTER IV

THE DUTIES OF THE BEST MAN

In all but the most quiet of weddings, the duties of the best man are many. It might almost be said that the success of the proceedings depends upon him more than upon any other single individual. Although he is nominally no more than a supporter of the bridegroom, he is in reality far more, for he is the one who must see that every necessary step has been taken in the proper manner, and that nothing has been forgotten.

His duties will commence almost as soon as the future bride has fixed the date of the wedding, and decided upon the form that the ceremony is to take. At the earliest moment, he should get to know what the fortunate couple have in view, and it is advisable that he should meet the two young people and quietly talk over the arrangements.

At the ceremony there will be many small duties that need attention, and it is a good plan for the best man to get in touch with a few friends of the groom, and enlist them as groomsmen. They could show visitors to their seats in church, to their cars after the service, assist the bridesmaids, and in many ways ease the strain on the best man.

Although it is not necessary, it is certainly a good idea for him to go with the bridegroom to the church, registrar's office, or other official place, to make the first intimation of the forthcoming wedding. The bridegroom, on this occasion, is seldom in the frame of mind to act in the most business-like manner; he may easily omit to mention necessary facts, and it is here that the best man steps in for the first time and shows how well his official title suits him.

The first step having been taken, the other arrangements follow in rapid succession, and in a more or less natural sequence. It will be advisable, when the wedding is to take place in a church or chapel, for the best man to lose no time in discussing the arrangements with the vestry clerk. Such matters are (1) whether the service is to be choral, and if so, when the hymns and wedding march may be discussed with the organist; (2) whether the altar is to be decorated florally, and if so, who will do it and when it ought to be done; and (3) what fees have to be paid to the choir—all these important questions must be fully dealt with by the best man at the earliest possible date.

Although it is not absolutely one of his duties, it is just as well for the best man to give an eye to the invitations. These may occasion a good deal of clerical work, and it will be a kindly act if he offers to assist the bride's mother in getting them out promptly.

His next duty will be to see to the cars that will be wanted for the actual day. He must consult the bride's father on this point, but, as it is the custom for the latter to pay for those which will take the company from the house to the church and back, it often happens that the father attends to this item himself. Nevertheless, the best man must be quite certain that the cars have been properly booked. In any case, he will have to engage the car that carries the bridegroom to the church, and, probably, the one that is used by the newly married couple when they leave home for the honeymoon. But nowadays, when nearly everyone has a car of his own, friends can be asked to transport guests thus keeping the number of hired cars to the minimum.

Another duty of the best man is to give the bridegroom assistance with his clothes. Also, he may be required to buy gloves, ties, collars, and other odds and ends, not only needed for the ceremony, but for the honeymoon. It is quite likely that he will be asked to buy suitable presents for the bridesmaids.

As the time draws near, the best man will run over his duties, in his mind, and see that he has forgotten nothing. Above all he will make quite sure that the bridegroom is in possession of the ring and the necessary documents. For instance, if the bride and bridegroom live in different districts, and it is a marriage by banns, has the certificate of the distant clergyman been obtained? According to the form of marriage, so the required documents will vary. As full particulars on this point are given in the chapter entitled, *How to get Married*, it will be wise to read it through.

Late in the day before the actual event, the best man will do well to call on the bridegroom. Whether he has any final instructions to give him or not, the call should not be neglected, seeing that there is always a chance that something important may need consideration.

When the eventful day arrives, the best man must bestir himself early, especially if the ceremony is fixed for any hour before two o'clock. After he has attended to his own equipment, which should be more or less similar to that of the bridegroom, he calls on the latter, helps him to dress and then drives with him to the church. Before leaving the house, he makes himself responsible for all the documents and the all-important ring.

On arrival at the church, the two walk unconcernedly to the chancel, and there await the bride. When she appears in company with her father, or chief friend in his place, the gathering falls into correct position, according to the instructions given in the chapter headed, *The Wedding Arrangements*. Here it may be well to repeat that the bridegroom stands on the right of the bride, the best man on the right side of the bridegroom, and a little to the rear. The best man can prompt the bridegroom if he is nervous during the service.

When the service is over, and the bridal pair proceed to the vestry, the best man then gives his arm to the chief bridesmaid, and the two follow the wedded couple and their parents. He usually signs the register.

Afterwards, he goes with the procession to the porch, and arranges how the various members of the party are to drive back to the house. The correct order has already been set out in the chapter entitled, *The Wedding Arrangements*.

In his spare moments, he tenders the arranged fees to the clergy, the choirmaster, and leaves gratuities for the church hands. Then he proceeds to the reception in the last car.

During the "breakfast," he invariably stands up and makes some congratulatory remarks in favour of the happy couple. If the gathering is of a formal nature, the speech properly allotted to him is the reply to the toast to the health of the bridesmaids. His speech should be of a light-hearted, good-natured character.

When the newly married couple set off for the honeymoon, the best man usually proceeds to the railway station and bids them "good-bye." With this pleasant task, his duties come to an end.

Naturally the best man is repaid his outlays by the bridegroom; but the "settling up" of these expenses is usually postponed until the happy pair have returned from their honeymoon.

CHAPTER V

THE DUTIES OF THE CHIEF BRIDESMAID

THE duties of the chief bridesmaid are of an exacting character; but most of her work takes the form of helping the bride before the event, and waiting on her during the ceremony.

Set out in detail, her duties may be described as follows:

(1) She should discuss the question of dresses with the bride, including those of the bridesmaids, who are arrayed closely alike. Their gowns should be chosen to harmonize in character and colour with those of the bride, if she is not in white. The bride must be consulted before the frocks are put in hand.

(2) If asked, she should be prepared to assist in purchasing various of the smaller things needed for the wedding and the new home.

(3) On the wedding day, she will wait on the bride while dressing, if asked to do so, but she will proceed to the church in a car in advance of the bride.

(4) At the church, she follows behind the bride and her father as they proceed up the aisle.

(5) She then takes up her position on the bride's left

and a little to the rear, ready to hold the bouquet, attend to the veil, if worn, and take the bride's glove when it is removed for the ring, if the bride is wearing gloves.

(6) When the bride and bridegroom proceed to the vestry to sign the register, she follows before the parents and near relations, on the arm of the best man.

(7) When the married couple return to the cars, she follows them to the porch.

(8) At the breakfast or reception, the chief bridesmaid is constantly at the bride's elbow ready to perform any little service.

(9) When the bride retires to change into her going-away dress, she is again in attendance.

(10) Often, it is the chief bridesmaid who welcomes the happy couple to their new home, when the honeymoon is at an end.

CHAPTER VI

WEDDING TOASTS AND SPEECHES

ALTHOUGH speeches are usually unnecessary at wedding celebrations, and toasts are best when short and to the point, there is no doubt that some receptions would be incomplete without these essays of oratory. For such occasions, the following hints and specimens will be found particularly useful.

TOAST TO THE BRIDE AND BRIDEGROOM

If ever a speech should be brief, it is this one. Time is needed for more important diversions, but the "health" must be proposed, and the specimen given here will take but three minutes to deliver. It is necessary to remind some speakers that the married couple are probably feeling their position, and that unpleasant allusions will add considerably to their embarrassment. Such remarks should be omitted.

"Ladies and Gentlemen—The making of speeches is an art of which I have little experience, but I feel impelled to call your attention to a little ceremony which I think we ought not to omit. Before we speed them on their journey, we must drink a bumper toast to the happy pair who have today embarked upon a great adventure. Of late we have heard much in regard to the matrimonial adventure —we have been told that it is going out of fashion, that it is a lottery in which the prizes are all blanks, and much more to the same effect; but I am inclined to think that the explanation of these vapourings is that they emanate from the bridegroom's unsuccessful rivals. For there is no doubt in my mind that he has secured a prize, and that she, in her turn, has by no means drawn a blank. They agree with, you see—observe it in their faces! Ladies and gentlemen, let us drink to the long life, prosperity, and, above all, the happiness of the Bride and Groom."

The following quotations may be found useful for including in a speech of this character:

Thy wife is a constellation of virtues; she is moon, and thou are the man in the moon.

Congreve.

The first year of marriage is always an adjustment—the rest is the same thing.

Across the threshold led,
And ev'ry tear kissed off as soon as shed,

His home she enters, there to be a light,
Shining within, when all without is night.

Rogers.

Reply by the Bridegroom

As a rule, the bridegroom's reply is brief; indeed it often consists of no more than a few suitable words of thanks. Nobody expects a flow of oratory from him on this occasion. If he should feel disposed to deliver a regular speech, such as the following, he must go warily. While he can say what a fortunate man he considers himself, he must avoid giving a list of the bride's good qualities; but he can mention how considerately the members of her family have always treated him. The moment is a good one to put such a fact on record. If the bride feels disposed, she may rise and make a remark or two, but, as a rule, she remains silent or just says, "You've all been very kind, and I thank you ever so much."

"Ladies and Gentlemen—I thank you all for your kind thoughts. With so many warm friends, I fail to see why we should ever lack the happiness you wish us. For whatever may be in store for us, if we are to experience some of the trials and troubles that are mankind's common lot, I am sure that friendship such as yours will enable us to meet them with courage and surmount them with success. In thanking you again, on behalf of my wife and myself, for your kindly good wishes, I wish to express my gratitude especially to the ladies who have supported my wife in her trying ordeal—which, however, I secretly believe, she has enjoyed thoroughly.—Ladies and Gentlemen, thank you very much indeed."

The following quotations will prove helpful in making a personally-composed speech:

. . . . My dear, my better half!—*Sir Philip Sydney.*

Man's best possession is a sympathetic wife.
Congreve.

Marriage must be a relation either of sympathy or of conquest.—*George Eliot.*

A nation stands or falls with the sanctity of its domestic ties.—*Robertson.*

As unto the bow the cord is,
So unto the man is woman;
Though she bends him, she obeys him,
Though she draws him yet she follows—
Useless each without the other!
Longfellow.

Love's history is not ended by marriage.—
Bayard Taylor.

The Health of the Bridesmaids

This is by no means an easy speech to make, as there

is so little real matter on which to rely. A few congratulatory remarks must form the basis of the theme, and these coupled with some topical suggestions, will help the speaker to complete his short oration. In many cases, this toast is proposed by the bridegroom as part of his speech.

"Ladies and Gentlemen—I have a very pleasant duty to perform, and that is to propose the health of the bridesmaids. On such an occasion as this, we are liable to centre our chief thoughts on the bride and bridegroom, but I know that these two fortunate people will not begrudge a little of your enthusiasm for the ladies who have acted as bridesmaids. Their work may not appear very arduous, but, personally I think it is, and I am sure you will all agree with me when I say that they have performed the duties admirably. The bride assures me that Miss (the chief bridesmaid) has given her a considerable amount of assistance in selecting and arranging the things for the new home, and I am bold enough to hope that Miss —— will, at no distant date, have to plan a home of her very own. In fact, my advice to all the bridesmaids is to follow the example of the happy bride at the very first opportunity. I see by your smiles that you all agree fully with my sentiments. That being so, I will conclude my remarks with the 'Health of the Bridesmaids'."

In composing other speeches, similar to the above, the following quotations may be aptly used:

The woman that deliberates is lost.—
Addison.

All thoughts, all passions, all delights,
Whatever stirs this mortal frame,
Are all but ministers of Love,
And feed his sacred flame.—*Coleridge.*

Nature intended that woman should be her masterpiece.—*Lessing.*

The Best Man Replies to the Toast of the Bridesmaids

The best man must attend closely to the speech proposing the toast of the bridesmaids, for it will help him with suggestions for his own speech. Here again, there is very little real matter on which to dwell, and his sheet anchor will be a few congratulatory remarks, coupled with any topical tit-bit which he can glean from the ceremony.

"Ladies and Gentlemen—At a wedding, nobody takes much notice of the men—the bridegroom excepted, of course. That being so, I'm afraid very few people appreciate how onerous my duties were. The best man has, in my opinion, the hardest task of all, for he has to keep an eye not only on the bridegroom, but on all the bridesmaids. I rather appreciated my task, however, because—well, look at the bridesmaids! I read in a fashion book the other day that weddings are being celebrated more and more without bridesmaids. My only hope is that the book was wrong, for what a joy they impart to the proceedings! A bachelor, as I am, is apt at first to feel that nothing is worth while once the bridegroom has carried off his bride; but the bridesmaids do help to revive our interest in the fair sex. It is because of the radiance they shed on the proceedings that I heartily agree with the proposer of the toast. In conclusion, may I say on behalf of the bridesmaids, thank you very much."

The following quotations may prove useful:

Of all actions of a man's life, his marriage does least concern other people; yet of all actions of our life, 'tis most meddled with by other people.—
Table Talk.

Well-married, a man is winged; ill-matched he is shackled.—*Beecher.*

The most precious possession that ever comes to a man in this world is a woman's heart.—*Holland.*

CHAPTER VII

THE SECOND MARRIAGE

The general details supplied in Chapter III should be studied in conjunction with this chapter, as the following information refers only to the differences that concern a second or subsequent marriage.

A WIDOW, on remarrying, has no legal formalities to attend to other than those set down in the chapter entitled *How to Get Married.* There are, however, certain rules of etiquette which she should observe specially.

First, she may send out the invitations in her own name and be married from her own house; but this is not a usual course. Generally, a widow begs a friend to chaperone her on the occasion; then the friend issues the invitations and holds the reception. The invitation, in such a case, is worded as follows:

"Dr. and Mrs. Smith request the pleasure of Mr. and Mrs. Robinson's company at the marriage of Mrs. Arthur Wordsworth with Dr. Bertram Hicks at All Saints' Church, Belgravia, S.W.1, on 15 May, at

2.15 p.m., and afterwards at 609 Victoria Street, S.W.1."

At the ceremony, the widow does not wear a white robe, nor a bridal veil, as these are reserved for maidenhood. Any other colours may be chosen; but mauve, lilac or smoke grey are most popular. She has no bridesmaids nor pages, in the usual sense; but if a lady friend supports her at the altar, and during the festivities, this lady is known as a maid of honour.

Her former ring must be removed before proceeding to the church, or the registrar's office. As a matter of courtesy, she should not wear it again unless expressly permitted by the second husband. If the permission is granted, the proper place for this first ring is on the same finger of the left hand, but above the new ring.

There is no reason why a widow should not have a bride cake at the second wedding, nor is there any reason for omitting to invite relatives of the first husband to the function, if they are on friendly terms.

These suggestions apply equally to a woman who has been divorced, or who has divorced her previous husband.

CHAPTER VIII

THE HONEYMOON AND AFTERWARDS

THE wedding ceremony and reception, as we have seen, need careful thought and planning. So does the first trip that the newly married couple take together. Most people will want to have a honeymoon and the traditional method of starting on honeymoon immediately after the wedding ceremony is still followed by the majority of couples who get married nowadays.

Apart from considerations of cost, the most important factor is to take a honeymoon which will appeal to both husband and wife. A honeymoon in which the interests of one partner are followed while the other trails along with the minimum of interest or enthusiasm is not a propitious way to start married life. So there should be a thorough discussion well before the wedding—and, most important of all, everything should be booked up well in advance. It would be unpardonable to leave arrangements to chance. Neither should a honeymoon last too long—otherwise the wife will long to be in her new home and their financial resources will be strained.

It would be out of place to give a detailed list of

places to visit on honeymoon as not only do individual tastes vary but the fashion in honeymoon resorts changes. So we will confine ourselves to giving a few suggestions. The young couple can visit their local travel agent to get full details of all the exciting places they can visit either in Europe or in the British Isles.

One of the favourite places for honeymoon couples is Majorca in the Balearic Islands. Others like to go to Italy or southern Spain where they can enjoy the sun. Those who like a leisurely honeymoon can go on a cruise. Paris is another favourite spot. It is equally suitable for a winter honeymoon.

For those who prefer to stay in the British Isles London is chosen by many couples. Like Paris, it is a good place for a winter honeymoon and for those who do not relish the prospect of finding themselves completely alone at some lonely beauty spot where walking and fishing are the only amusements available. Devon and Cornwall are favourite parts of the country to visit, other couples like to tour cathedrals and abbeys. This sort of honeymoon is especially suitable for the many that take their own car with them when they go.

But the detailed choice must, in the end, be left to the couple concerned. Should either party be interested in photography the camera should be included in the luggage, so that a permanent record of the trip can be made. They should cater for their own interests and should they be golf or tennis enthusiasts should take golf clubs and their tennis rackets with them. Neither should they economize with their luggage. With so many couples going on holiday in their own car the problem of luggage is less than when people travelled exclusively by train. But remember that if you are travelling by air that you will be charged excess if your luggage is above a certain weight.

In recent years there has been a tendency to take the honeymoon some time after the wedding. Until marriage the couple have seen each other for hours or perhaps a day at a time, rarely more. Many people feel that they can get to know each other better if they do this in their own home. After all the emotional turmoil of the weeks before the wedding and the strain of the great day itself, the young bride in particular does need a few worry-free days. She may well feel disconcerted to find herself staying in a strange place with a semi-stranger. Marriage represents a completely new phase in one's life. Two adults who have already developed personality and ways of their own have to learn to adjust themselves to each other. The old cliché of give and take is just as relevant as ever it was, but it is not always easy to put into practice. The first few weeks of marriage are not without their problems in spite of the general aura of happiness and wonder. So some couples will enjoy the honeymoon much more if it is delayed as they can get to know each other better in the meantime and can therefore enjoy the journey to the full. So they will just have a few days break after the wedding, or even none at all, and take the honeymoon later. This is an especially good idea if the wedding takes place in the winter and the couple want a honeymoon in the country and prefer not to go to a large city like London or Paris. But just as with the choice of place for the honeymoon, the final decision as to when it is taken can only be left to the husband and wife themselves.

In a later chapter we point out that of necessity when the young couple have children they are unable to travel for many years until the children are older. Even if they can travel, their journeys are restricted. The wife is even more restricted than the husband as few people are in the fortunate position of being able to afford a full-time nurse to look after their children as was done in years gone by. Many women do not want to do this in any case, even if they can afford it.

So it is vitally important that the couple have a honeymoon and that the husband realizes that for many wives, it is not only an exciting and romantic experience but the last carefree holiday she will have for many years. There must be no feeling, at some future date, that one or other was robbed, through some misunderstanding of the most enjoyable holiday trip of his or her life.

CHAPTER IX

THE BEST AGE AT WHICH TO MARRY

WHAT is the best age at which to marry?

The question cannot be answered in a definite manner, since everybody is, more or less, a law unto him or herself. One individual will point to a supremely happy couple, and say, "Look at Mr. and Mrs. X. They married in their teens. That's evidently the time to get married." Another person will instance the case of Mr. and Mrs. Y. "No husband and wife could be more fond of each other than they are," he will affirm, and then add, "But, of course, they didn't rush into a hasty union. He was forty and she thirty-five when he led her to the altar."

Such cases as these prove nothing, except that some fortunate people are born to be happy, and, however much they depart from the normal, they will still be happy. What we want to discuss here is the best age for the *average* person to marry.

Clearly, getting married is an affair which involves certain questions of finance. It is no use to argue that a man should be such and such an age; a woman so many years his junior, and then to admit that at that particular age the man cannot afford to support a wife. The money side of the question cannot be ignored, and it is a matter to be considered as much by the girl as by the man.

One conclusion may be drawn from this statement that money counts. It is this—if a man reaches his maximum capacity for earning at an early age, he may reasonably marry early; while if he attains his highest point late in life, then marriage for him must be delayed.

Thus it comes about that a navvy may marry much earlier than a medical practitioner, a motor mechanic long before a barrister.

Of course, it is folly for a man to shoulder the responsibilities of married life before he has made a certain amount of headway and gained a position of some security in the world. Not only is it folly, but it has often turned out to be criminal, as well.

Neither should a man or a woman marry until their desire to travel has lessened. Even today, with travel by the masses, a family of small children are difficult to travel with. The first ten or fifteen years of family life are, of necessity, very static, with travel restricted to the annual pilgrimage to the seaside and day trips in the family car.

The desire for security can be carried too far. There is not the slightest doubt that, when the right woman is chosen, she will often be the means of spurring on her husband to higher flights of ambition. Many a man is prepared to admit that his successes are due to the fact that he has a wife who gives him the courage and the vision to get on. When such a wife is possessed, it hardly matters when a man marries. Similarly, children can be left with "in-laws" or a nurse, while the parents travel.

Looking at all the factors squarely, we think that, for a man of good education, who is in possession of a post of fair average security, the best age to marry is twenty-five or twenty-six. A year earlier, or a year or two later, hardly make any difference. Although for some people a late marriage is much more successful.

For a girl, the best is twenty-one or twenty-two. These figures are arrived at in the following way: Take the man's age, halve it, and then add eight. This formula may be used not only in the above case, but it will tell a man of almost any age how old should be his chosen spouse. Thus a man of fifty is advised to wed a woman of thirty-three, and a man of thirty, a girl of twenty-three.

While the man's point of view is largely one of finance and mobility the girl's is entirely different.

Her natural desire is to have a home and raise a family as soon as she can. However, nowadays when young people earn such high wages girls are often reluctant to give up lucrative jobs which make the first years of marriage so much less of a financial strain.

Many couples today, especially those who marry very young, decide not to have a family for, say, five or six years and concentrate on working themselves up into a good financial position. Often the wife takes part-time work when her children are at school and returns to a full-time career when her children are grown up. There is much to be said for this, though the argument that when the wife works there is no home life for the children is equally convincing. In the end it can only be decided by the couple themselves after the financial and all other considerations are taken into account.

CHAPTER X

MARRIAGE SYMBOLS AND SIGNS

DESPITE the commercialism of today marriage customs and superstitions survive to bring colour into what is often a grey, drab world.

Take, for instance, the ring. An Act of Parliament passed as far back as the year 1837 expressly stated that a marriage could legally take place without it. Legally, yes; but would sentiment and custom forgo this tiny hoop of gold? A registrar supplies the answer. He states that only twice in a long experience has he officiated at a wedding when the ring was purposely banished.

As a symbol of marriage, the wedding ring dates back to heathen times, when all contracts were ratified by one party giving the other a ring to signify that he agreed to the bargain. Its shape and conception have been explained by a long forgotten writer, who claimed that "the ring is made of gold to show how noble and durable are our affections; the form is round to imply that our regards shall never have an end, and the place of it is on the third finger of the left hand, whence the ancients thought there was a vein which came directly from the heart."

This idea that the third finger and the heart were intimately connected is anatomically incorrect; but the supposition seems to be such a charming piece of sentiment that it is almost a pity to give the correct reason, which is far more prosaic. It is simply this: the third finger was chosen because it is used less than any other, and because it is protected by the surrounding fingers. Thus the ring is comparatively immune from wear and danger, when worn in the position long decreed by custom.

Another symbol connected with weddings is the veil worn by the bride. If we go back to very ancient times, it will be found that the two parties of the marriage were enshrouded in a canopy of flimsy material, in order that their faces might be screened from the gaze of the curious. Today, the groom has lost his share of the covering, presumably because he can endure the ordeal with equanimity; but the bride wears her portion in the shape of a veil, if she is so minded.

Frequently, the bride carries a bouquet, looking upon it as something merely ornamental to her person. But it is more than that; for centuries ago, it formed part of a wreath, and, in bygone times, wreaths were worn to typify several great occasions, marriage being only one of them.

The orange blossom which the bride wears was originally grown in the Holy Land, where it was a sign of purity, innocence and religious observance.

The confetti thrown at the church door, after the ceremony, is a modern substitute for rice. Rice was a symbol of happiness because it betokened a full harvest. Thus, the people who scatter confetti or rice over the newly-married couple are expressing a hope that the two will never suffer from want; but enjoy a lavish share of this world's goods.

Still another custom connected with weddings is to throw an old shoe after the happy pair, or to tie one to the going-away baggage. Why an old shoe should be thought to bring good luck is a little obscure. In Anglo-Saxon weddings, it was the custom for the father of the bride to give one of his daughter's shoes to the newly-wedded husband, and the latter, on receiving it, touched his wife with the tip of the sole in order to make it quite clear that he was her lord and master. Viewed in this light, there seems nothing to recommend the introduction of an old shoe into the weddings of today.

The bride cake is yet another symbol of the marriage festivities which requires an explanation. It originated through the Romans, whose brides always ate a portion of a cake made of flour and water, as a sign that they hoped they would never lack the simple necessaries of life. Out of this humble fare has grown the elaborate bride cake of today.

CHAPTER XI

WEDDING DAY SUPERSTITIONS

It is not surprising that so important an event as a wedding should be surrounded by a number of superstitions, seldom, if ever, founded on any show of reason.

Colours. Here is a well-known rhyme that touches on the important subject of the colour of the bride's attire.

Married in white,
She has chosen aright.
Married in blue,
Her love will be true.
Married in yellow,
She'll be ashamed of the fellow.
Married in red,
She'll wish herself dead.
Married in black,
She'll wish herself back.
Married in grey,
She'll travel far away.
Married in pink,

And her spirits will sink.
Married in green,
She'll be ashamed to be seen.

The following colour interpretations are calculated to be more correct, and for several centuries they have been accepted as faithful portents—more or less—of the future.

White is a symbol of purity and of high virtues.

Green typifies youth, hope and happiness.

Red is a sign of vigour, courage and great passion. There may be a touch of jealousy in its reading, however.

Violet denotes dignity, pride, and a condition of high ideals.

Some of the above ideas are incorporated in the old jingle which claims that the bride should wear:

Something old and something new,
Something borrowed, something blue.

TIME. Much importance has always been attached, by the superstitious minded, to the day of the week chosen for a marriage. The following verse puts these views in a nutshell:

Monday for health,
Tuesday for wealth;

Wednesday, the best day of all.
Thursday for losses,
Friday for crosses;
Saturday, no luck at all!

When it is remembered that more people marry on Saturdays than on all the other days of the week put together, it seems almost a pity that the above lines are not better known—that is, if they have any truth in them at all.

Just as important as the day, is the month chosen for the wedding, if the rhyme quoted below is to be taken seriously.

Married in January's frost and rime,
Widow's you'll be before your time.
Married in February's cruel weather,
Life you'll walk in tune together.
Married when March winds blow and roar,
Your home will be on some foreign shore.
Married 'neath April's changeful skies,
A chequered path before you lies.
Married in May when the honey bees flit,
Strangers around your table will sit.
Married during the month of June,
Life will be one long honeymoon.
Married in July when the flowers are ablaze,
Bittersweet memories in after days.

Married in August's heat and drowse,
Lover and friend in your chosen spouse.
Married in September's autumn glow,
Smooth and serene your life will flow.
Married when October leaves grow thin,
Toil and hardship for both begin.
Married in November's month of mist,
Fortune your wedding ring has kissed.
When December's snow fall fast,
The marriage is happy and love will last.

To go a step further, we may claim, on the authority of an astrologer of note, that the following days are especially lucky for weddings:

January	2	4	11	19	21	
February	1	3	10	19	21	
March	3	5	12	20	23	
April	2	4	12	20	22	
May	2	4	12	20	23	
June	1	3	11	19	21	
July	1	3	12	19	21	31
August	2	11	18	20	30	
September	1	9	16	18	28	
October		15	18	27	29	
November	5	11	13	22	25	
December	1	8	10	19	23	29

Against the above, we may place the following dates which are particularly unlucky:

January 29; February 8, 11, 17; April 16, 21; May 15, 26; June 4, 8; July 15, 23; August 19, 24; September 6, 7; November 15, 20; December 6, 7, 9.

Miscellaneous Omens

Most of the superstitions affecting weddings are of a mixed character, touching upon all sorts of complex things. We would give prior place, however, to the saying that "Happy is the bride whom the sun shines on," because, after all, a ray of sunshine can transform a gloomy picture into one of radiant splendour. The sun being so necessary, it follows that a bride will not welcome the rain. Now, if she has no desire for rain, her course is easy should there be a cat in the house. All she has to do is to feed the creature with her own hands on the wedding morn. The cat, having the powers of propitiating the elements, will then look kindly on her act and see to it that no rain falls.

Speaking of cats, it is well to mention that if a black cat is seen while on the way to the church, good luck is sure to come of it, while for a black cat to rub against the bride, is the height of good fortune.

But to return to the question of rain, for a moment; it is very certain that most British brides prefer their chosen day to be favoured by its absence, yet her sister in Germany goes to the extent of praying for rain, since in the Fatherland each drop is looked upon as a precious blessing bringing with it some added joy.

If the bride is wakened on her wedding morn by the song of a bird, even though it is only the chirping of a sparrow, she may accept that as a good augury; also, if she discovers a spider in the folds of her dress—an unlikely thing, unless put there by the kind agency of a friend—the results will be all to the good.

It is usually agreed that to break anything on the momentous morning, especially a mirror, is a bad sign, and it is equally disconcerting to lose the heel of a shoe.

While mentioning mirrors, it may be said that it is highly necessary for the bride to add something to her toilet at every fresh glance into a looking glass, even if it is only her gloves. After the ceremony, it augers well for their happiness if the happy pair look by chance into a mirror together; but all the good is undone if the act is planned beforehand.

It is a decidedly bad piece of luck for the two young people to meet on the morning of the wedding before the ceremony; but it is equally fortunate if they smile on each other as they meet at the altar.

A bride is not supposed to weep before marriage, but she may do so to her heart's content after the actual ceremony—and thus prove that she is no witch, as the latter could only shed three tears from her left eye!

If the bride sees a lamb, a dove, a spider, a toad, or a black cat, already mentioned, when on her way to the church, then these are emblems of good luck; but it is reckoned as a very bad omen if she should encounter a funeral party, because it portends that somebody is bound to die soon. A pig that crosses the road in front of the wedding car has a similar effect.

After the wedding, the bridal bouquet should be broken up and tossed among the bridesmaids and girl friends. Whoever catches these fragments is expected to enter upon the marriage state at no very distant date.

On changing her wedding toilet for her going-away gown, a bride should remove all the pins, and either throw them away or toss them, as she did the bouquet, to her friends, otherwise bad luck is sure to attend her.

Few superstitions concern themselves with the conduct of the bridegroom on his wedding day. All will be well so long as he does not see his bride in bridal attire before he meets her at the altar, does not let his hat fall, does not drop the ring or put it only partially on his bride's finger. If she has to assist him in this matter, then he may expect to be ruled by her in the future. He should fee the clergyman (through the best man) with an odd sum of money, carry a small mascot in his pocket, and on no account must he turn back for anything after the wedding journey has once started.

At the homecoming, after the honeymoon, it is

imperative that the husband carries his wife across or over the threshold of their new home. When this is done, both will be blessed with all the good fortune they desire.

CHAPTER XII

VITAL MATTERS FOR EVERY HUSBAND

GETTING married is an important matter, especially when considered from the legal aspect. In this department, nothing is more vital than the husband's will. Unless it is in order on, at latest, the very day of the marriage, the wife is placed in a false position to which she should not be subjected.

As a rule, the husband will bequeath all, or the major part of his possessions, to his wife, and, when this is done, it is only reasonable that the wife, also, should lose no time in making a will, bequeathing her property, similarly, to her husband.

Formerly, a will made before marriage was revoked on marriage; but, by the Law of Property Act, 1925, a will drawn up in contemplation of such a union is in perfect order if the wording makes this fact absolutely clear. Since the best time to draw up a will is a short while before "the day," and not on the day itself, it is necessary to know how to express this contemplative idea. The following form of wording may be followed safely:

FORM OF WILL MADE IN CONTEMPLATION OF MARRIAGE

This is the last will of me Thomas Askew of 477 Old Palace Lane Richmond in the County of Surrey Banker made in contemplation of my marriage with Joan Bellamy of 366 The Green Richmond in the County of Surrey spinster I appoint the said Joan Bellamy sole executrix of this my will And I devise and bequeath all my property unto her absolutely In witness whereof I have hereunto set my hand this sixteenth day of March One thousand nine hundred and sixty-seven.

(Signed) Thomas Askew.

Signed by the above named Thomas Askew as his last will in the presence of us both present at the time who at his request in his presence and in the presence of each other have hereunto subscribed our names as witnesses.

Arthur Lightfoot,
115 Park Lane, Richmond, Surrey.
(Actor.)
Geoffrey Basing,
38 The Drive, Richmond, Surrey.
(Minister in Holy Orders.)

Note the absence of punctuation in the body of the will and note also that legal phraseology is avoided.

It is always better to use simple wording that can be understood than sentences evolved with a legal bias that may not mean exactly what is intended.

Making a Will on the Wedding Day

Although a prospective husband is advised to attend to his will some little time before the wedding day, it is quite certain that many procrastinators will put off the uninteresting task until the day itself. This, of course, is better than leaving it until some even later date. But the important question will then arise: Was the will made before the ceremony or after? Of course, the date will not provide a clue. If before the ceremony, the legacies may go to A, B and C, but if after, to X, and Z.

In order to make it quite clear that the will was drawn up *after* the ceremony, when the husband and wife were joined in matrimony, the following, or similar words should be added after the usual attestation clause to be signed by the witnesses.

> "And which signature by the said Ivor Archer and subscription by us took place between the hours of three and four o'clock in the afternoon of Wednesday the twenty-second day of March One thousand nine hundred and sixty-seven immediately after the solemnization on that day of the ceremony of marriage between the said Ivor Archer and Belinda Jackson now his wife."

Form of Will for a Married Man Leaving Everything to his Wife

Some husbands will arrive home from the honeymoon and still find that the all-important will is not yet in actual being. They must not lose another moment. Two friends should be found forthwith, in order that their signatures may be appended to the following:

This is the last will of me David Shipman of 704 The Chase Rye in the County of Sussex Produce Broker I devise and bequeath all my property unto my wife Judith absolutely and I appoint her to be the sole executrix of this my will. In witness whereof I have hereunto set my hand this twenty-fourth day of April One thousand nine hundred and sixty-seven.

(Signed) David Shipman.

Signed by the above named David Shipman as his last will in the presence of us both at the same time who at his request and in his presence and in the presence of each other have hereunto subscribed our names as witnesses:

Kenneth Frazer,
17 The Long Drive, St. Albans, Hertfordshire.
(Schoolmaster.)

Bertram Goodchild,
414 High Street, Guildford, Surrey.
(Accountant.)

Insurances

Yet another matter that must be considered by the husband concerns the question of taking out a life insurance. From now onwards, the husband is a man who has responsibilities. Should he die without such provision, his wife would probably suffer financially, especially as most young couples have very little money left after the home has been got together. It is to safeguard her in the event of his death that the life policy is needed.

Of course, there are policies of all kinds, offering a multitude of different benefits, and it is often their bewildering array of terms that causes the young husband to put off definite action. He hardly knows which policy is best to take out, and refusing to leap in the dark he does nothing.

To shelve the matter is the greatest mistake that can be committed. For one thing, the years roll by with amazing rapidity and the older the husband grows, the more will be the annual premiums he will have to pay in order to secure reasonable benefits. And, of course, it is quite possible that he may die while he is still pondering over the best insurance to take up. His widow may then be left in a penniless condition.

So the first thing to do is to give the matter full and proper consideration without loss of time. If trustworthy friends cannot give such advice as is required, the best plan is to write to some of the best insurance companies and obtain from them the booklets which they publish. An enquiry of this kind will be sure to lead to visits by representatives of the company. It is advisable to listen to what these callers have to say and to keep an open mind throughout; but it is unwise to make promises before full deliberation has been made.

What most husbands require is a policy that is fully guaranteed the moment the first premium is paid. In other words, he does not want to have a probationary period of, say, three years before the benefits can be enforced. Secondly, he may not want a "whole life" policy so much as one which is fully paid up after a term of years. For instance, it may suit him better to have finished paying the premiums at, say, sixty than to be called upon to continue until death. Thirdly, he should avoid a policy that contains a number of restrictive clauses, which appear to mean nothing, but which may be, in fact, very detrimental.

Take the case of suicide. Many policies are void if the insured person ends his own life. Naturally, the young husband, full of the promise of the future, regards this as a thing that hardly concerns him. But what if he dies through an unfortunate street accident?

A case in point has come to our personal knowledge. A young husband was crossing a city thoroughfare when he was knocked down and killed. The driver of the motor realized that no blame would attach to him if he asserted that the man had deliberately walked in front of his engine, and the company in which the husband was insured quite legitimately withheld payment of the claim, in accordance with the terms in the policy, which rendered void their liability in the event of suicide of the Insured. The widow had the utmost difficulty in securing evidence to disprove the driver's statements, but, fortunately, she was successful in the end. If the husband's policy had not contained the clause relating to suicide, much worry and expense would have keen spared.

As to the amount for which the policy should be taken out, everything depends on the financial and social position of the married couple; but anything less than five hundred pounds is rarely of much use. A Rebate of Income Tax is granted on the premiums paid.

CHAPTER XIII

A HOUSE FOR THE MARRIED COUPLE

FROM necessity or choice, many couples live happily—and raise happy families—in rented houses or flats. Others prefer to own their houses, and it is for them that this chapter is written.

If you are going to have to take out a mortgage, this question divides itself into two parts: how much capital you can put down, and how much you expect to be able to pay out of your future income.

Unless you are a "sitting tenant" you are very unlikely to get a mortgage of more than 95 per cent. of the purchase price, and probably it will be less. You will have to pay the balance yourself. You will also have various legal and other expenses, and altogether you may assume that you will have to find at least 10 per cent. of the purchase price, probably more, in ready cash. This means, for example, that you are unlikely to be able to buy a £4,000 house unless you have £400 in the bank.

Whatever you borrow will have to be repaid in regular instalments; and your future outgoings will also include ground rent (if the house is leasehold), general and water rates, insurance premiums, and the cost of maintenance and repairs. The sum of these items should not exceed one-quarter of your basic income; in other words, one week's earnings should cover one month's outgoings on the cost of the house.

Lenders generally express their advances as percentages of the purchase price or of their valuation of the house—whichever is the lower. In the case of new houses the two figures are usually the same. If you are a "sitting tenant" in an old house the lender's valuation may even be higher than the purchase price. But otherwise it is almost certain that the lender's valuation will be lower (sometimes substantially) than the purchase price. So if you obtained, for example, an 80 per cent. mortgage on a house that cost £10,000, which the lender valued at £8,000, the loan would be £6,400, which is only 64 per cent. of the purchase price.

The chief lenders of money for house-purchase are local authorities, building societies, and assurance (or insurance) companies. The last two of these can be dealt with through mortgage brokers, who also have access to other funds.

Not all local authorities lend money for house-purchase. Local authorities are allowed to lend to persons buying houses outside their own areas, and in practice it is possible to obtain a mortgage from a local authority in nearly all parts of the country.

Local authorities are empowered to lend up to 90 per cent. of their own valuation of a house, so that unless you are a "sitting tenant" you will have to put down at least 10 per cent. yourself. Unless the house is new you will almost certainly have to put down more than that.

Local authorities may allow longer for repayment than other lenders. Some of them go up to thirty years or even longer. Usually, however, the rate of interest is lower for short loans than for the longer ones. This interest rate—which is fixed beforehand for the whole period of the loan—is sometimes lower than the rate charged by any other lender, and this often makes a local-authority mortgage the cheapest of the lot. The only disadvantages about borrowing from a local authority are that it usually takes a little longer to arrange the mortgage (but this is a minor inconvenience) and that it is not so easy to vary the terms later as it is with a building-society mortgage.

Most house-purchasers borrow from building societies, who usually give larger advances than other lenders. The normal advance is 80 per cent. (of the purchase or the society's valuation, whichever is the lower), but by taking out a mortgage indemnity policy or providing guarantees you may be able to get as much as 95 per cent.

Building societies usually lend for periods up to twenty-five years. Rates on interest may vary slightly from one society to another, but the majority charge the same. The rates may be higher than those charged by local authorities, but this depends entirely on government policy at the time. Building societies reserve the right to change the rate for old borrowers as well as new during the period of the loan. Building-society mortgages are exceptionally flexible, and their terms are most easily varied if, for example, the borrower is temporarily in financial difficulties.

Both local authorities and building societies generally arrange for the loan to be repaid in equal instalments of principal and interest combined. In practice this means that at the beginning each repayment consists mainly of interest, the proportion of principal increasing steadily as the loan is reduced. This does not affect the borrower at all. He has to pay the same monthly (or, less commonly, quarterly) instalments throughout the term of the loan.

There is an alternative method of repayment known as the fixed-instalment system, under which each repayment consists of a fixed amount of principal plus the interest due on the principal still outstanding at the time. This means that instalments are largest at the beginning of the loan and gradually decrease.

The third class of big lenders for house-purchase is

the life assurance (sometimes called insurance) companies. The system here is somewhat different, the mortgage loan being combined with an endowment assurance policy. This can be arranged either direct with an assurance company, which in that case will lend the money as well as give the assurance cover, or through a building society. Assurance companies normally advance up to 75 per cent. of the purchase price or the company's valuation, whichever is the lower. They will usually also advance the survey fee and the legal costs of the mortgage, including the stamp duty; but even with these additions the advance is not as much as the building societies' 80 per cent. Again, an additional advance can often be obtained by taking out a mortgage indemnity policy, but as a rule the top limit is 90 per cent.

Like local authorities—and unlike building societies—assurance companies lending money for house-purchase do not reserve the right to change the rate of interest for old borrowers, and so the rate remains the same for the whole period of the loan. The rate is usually the same as that charged by building societies at the time when the mortgage is taken out.

The main advantage of combining a mortgage with a life assurance policy is that it allows for greater relief of income tax. When you repay money borrowed from a local authority or a building society you are allowed tax relief on the interest but not on the principal of the loan. When you combine a mortgage with a life assurance, on the other hand, you do not repay the principal by instalments. You simply pay, again at regular intervals, the interest on the loan and the life-assurance premiums. The policy matures at the end of the term of the loan, and is then applied in repayment to clear the mortgage. If you die before the end of the term, the sum assured is applied in repayment then and again the mortgage is cleared. Under this system your gross payments will almost certainly be higher than they would be for the same loan from a building society, but your net expense may be less; because relief of income-tax is allowed on life-assurance premiums but not on repayments of the principal of a loan.

Generally speaking, the combination of a mortgage with endowment assurance is financially advantageous if you pay income tax at the full standard rate, but not otherwise. If your taxable income is not big enough for this—and not likely to be big enough in the future as far as you can foresee—you will be better off with a mortgage from a local authority or building society. Then, if you want to secure the house for your dependants in the event of your dying before the mortgage is cleared, you can take out a decreasing temporary assurance policy, which provides for the payment by the assurance company of a lump sum equivalent to the amount of the loan still outstanding at the time of your death. If you are borrowing from a building society, the society will usually arrange this for you, paying the full premium on your behalf and adding the sum to the loan so that this also is spread over the whole period of the mortgage. Building societies call this arrangement the "combined scheme." Local authorities do not offer any similar service, but assurance companies will usually agree to payment of the premiums in annual instalments.

If, however, you consider that your present or future liability for income tax makes the combination of the mortgage with an endowment assurance policy more attractive, you will not have to bother about this as the life cover will be automatic. One possible disadvantage of this method of borrowing is that it is less flexible than an ordinary mortgage, and it is not so easy to vary the terms of the loan. Also, if you sell the house before the end of the term, and therefore redeem the mortgage, you may suffer some financial loss that would not occur if you had borrowed from a local authority or building society.

There are other lenders for house-purchase besides local authorities, building societies, and assurance companies. Banks sometimes lend, usually only to their own customers; but they provide only short-term loans and reserve the right to call in the money when they want it. Solicitors sometimes have trust-funds for investment; again, the loan is usually for a shorter period than that allowed by the three big lenders, and it is unlikely to be as large a proportion of the purchase price. Interest is only charged (usually payable quarterly) until the loan is repaid at the end of the agreed term.

Finally, there are finance corporations and miscellaneous lenders who can usually be reached only through a mortgage broker.

Another question you will have to consider is whether to buy a house freehold or leasehold. The usual advice given on this subject is that it is always better to buy freehold. So it is; that is why it costs more. Obviously you will buy freehold if you can afford it, but you may have to choose between buying a good leasehold house and a not-so-good freehold house, the purchase price being the same for each. This is something you can only decide yourself, but bear in mind that when the lease expires, the house reverts to the owner of the land.

You will also have to consider whether to buy a new house or one that has already been occupied by someone else. The fact that a larger advance can usually be obtained on a new house has already been mentioned; and there are other obvious advantages. Most modern houses are better insulated against the winter than older houses, and are superior in other ways. But some rubbishy houses continue to be built, and unless you know something about the subject it is advisable, when buying a new house, to choose one that has been certified by the National House-Builders Registration Council. The Council keeps a National Register of reputable house-builders, and officers of the Council inspect houses under construction and on completion before issuing their certificate. You can get a list of the registered builders in your district by application to the National House-Builders Registration Council, 82 New Cavendish Street, London, W.1.

There is one other method of buying a house, and that is having it built to your own desires. If you decide to do this you should employ an architect to design it and supervise the building: if you cannot afford to do this you will probably be better off with a ready-made house put up by a builder on the National Register. You can get full information about architects' fees from the Royal Institute of British Architects, 66 Portland Place, London, W.1, which will also give you advice on finding an architect if you need it.

Most of the big lenders—except, as a rule, assurance companies—grant building mortgages, the advances being made in instalments as the work proceeds.

Whether you buy a ready-built house or build your own, you will have to conduct the transaction through a solicitor, and once you have put the matter in his hands you should not need to worry about suffering a loss through ignorance of the law. There is, however, one vital thing to bear in mind right at the start. When you agree to buy a house, or pay a deposit, do so "subject to contract," and insist on these important words being written on your receipt.

CHAPTER XIV

WEDDING ANNIVERSARIES

EVEN in these days of rapid movement and excitement, most people enjoy an occasional glance backwards to the past, and no such incident can affect us more vitally than the various milestones of our married life. To many of us, these are indeed happy memories, though to a few they may bring heart-ache and bitter thoughts.

Yet when it is a genuine case of Darby and Joan, what can be more beautiful, more wonderful, than the delightful exclamation: "Joan, darling, do you remember what happened thirty years ago today!"

Joan may pretend that housewifely cares and duties do not allow her to waste her time on such trifles, but in her inmost heart she is thrilled, because "her man" has remembered that long-distant day of glory when he placed the much-prized golden circlet on her finger! Dear, dear Darby—how good he has always been to her!

The recognition of the anniversaries tends to make life flow more smoothly, and married people should never fail to express some suitable wish to their chosen life-partner. It is a pleasant custom to make a suitable gift to mark the special year, and for this purpose, various articles have become associated with each individual year in the marriage series. The gift, therefore, should agree, as for instance, in the seventh year, when some present made of Wool should be chosen.

The following list gives the names generally associated with each year, but these vary slightly in some districts. For instance, Paper is given for the first year, Leather for the twelfth, Ivory for the thirtieth, Wool for the fortieth, and Silk for the forty-fifth.

1964	First Anniversary	Cotton Wedding
1965	Second „	Paper „
1966	Third „	Leather „
1968	Fifth „	Wooden „
1970	Seventh „	Woollen „
1973	Tenth „	Tin „
1976	Twelfth „	Silk and Fine Linen Wedding
1978	Fifteenth „	Crystal „
1983	Twentieth „	China „
1987	Twenty-fifth „	Silver „
1993	Thirtieth „	Pearl „
2003	Fortieth Anniversary	Ruby „
2013	Fiftieth „	Golden „
2023	Sixtieth or Seventy-	
2037	fifth Anniversaries	Diamond „

Nowadays, no special note is taken of most of these anniversaries; but the Silver and Golden weddings are exceptions. So also is the Diamond wedding, when such a rare event actually occurs. There is actually a record of a couple who spent over 100 years of married life together.

As a rule, when one of these anniversaries takes place, there is no better way of celebrating it than by arranging a dinner party, to which would be invited as many friends as possible who were actually present at the wedding. The event is an informal "happy memory" from the past, snatched from the turmoil and rush of life, so *intimacy*, not *formality*, should be the key-note of the proceedings.

For the more important anniversaries, such as the Silver or the Golden, some old friend might arrange a care-free gathering in a private room of some hotel; but, naturally, the "happy couple" would be consulted well in advance. In that case, they would be the guests of their friends, and would have nothing to do with the financial aspects of the gathering.

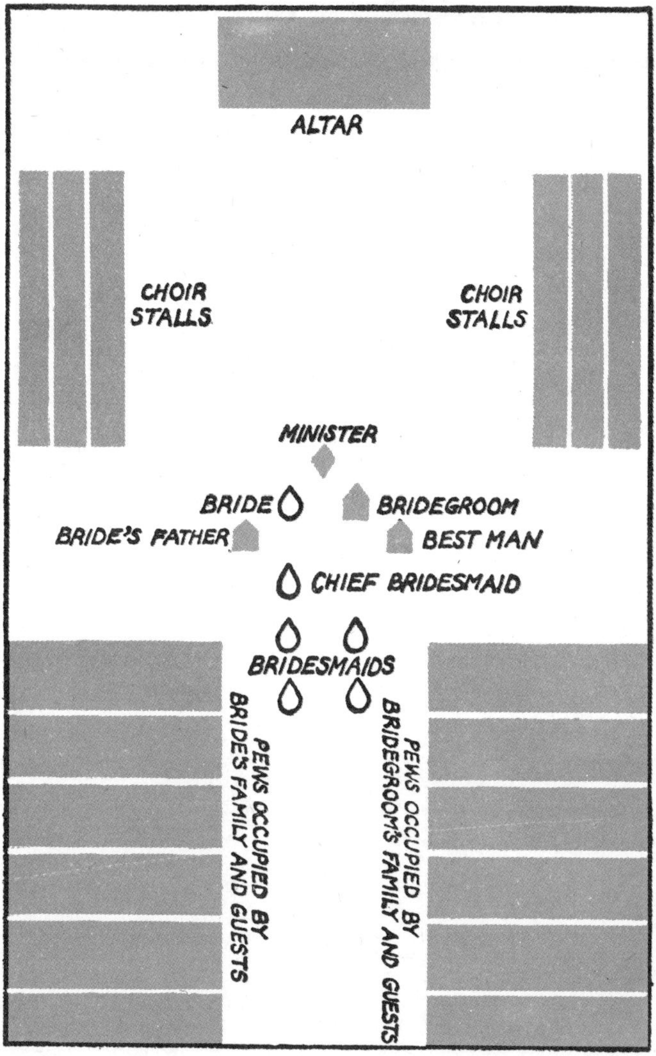

Fig. I. Grouping for the bethrothal, before the Chancel, during the first part of the Marriage Service.

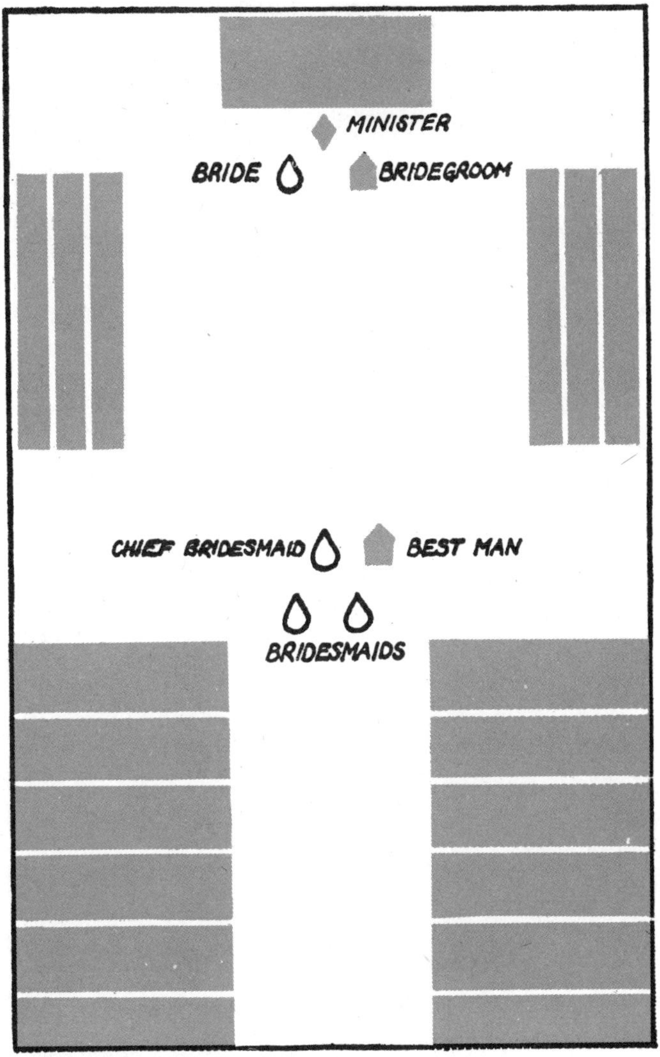

Fig. II. Grouping before the altar during the second part of the Marriage Service.

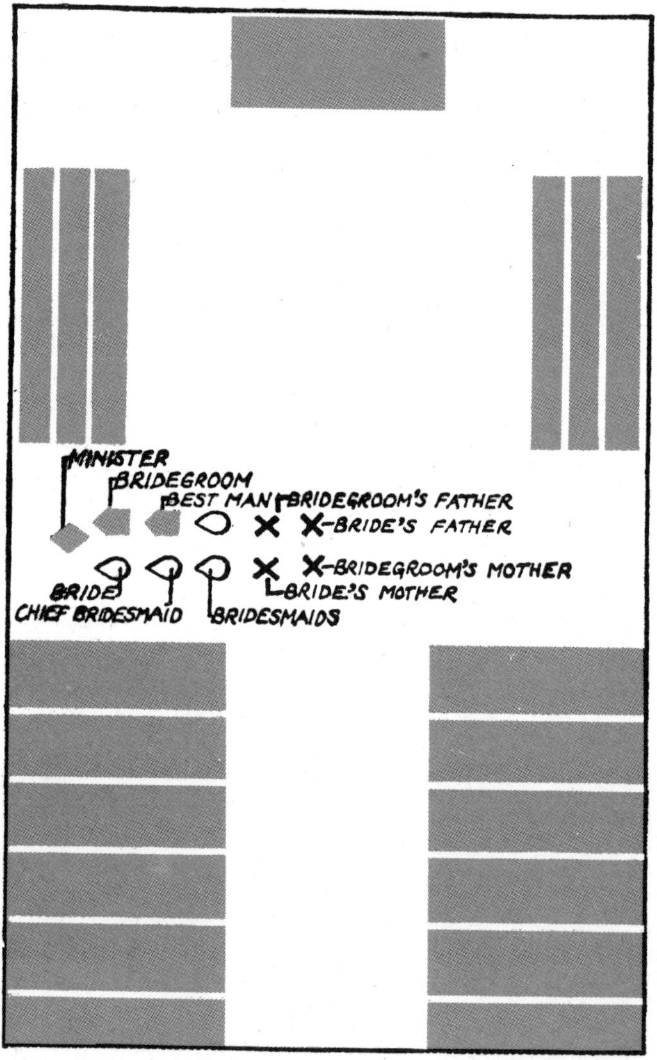

Fig. III. Grouping for the procession to the vestry. The same group formation without the minister, is used in the recessional.

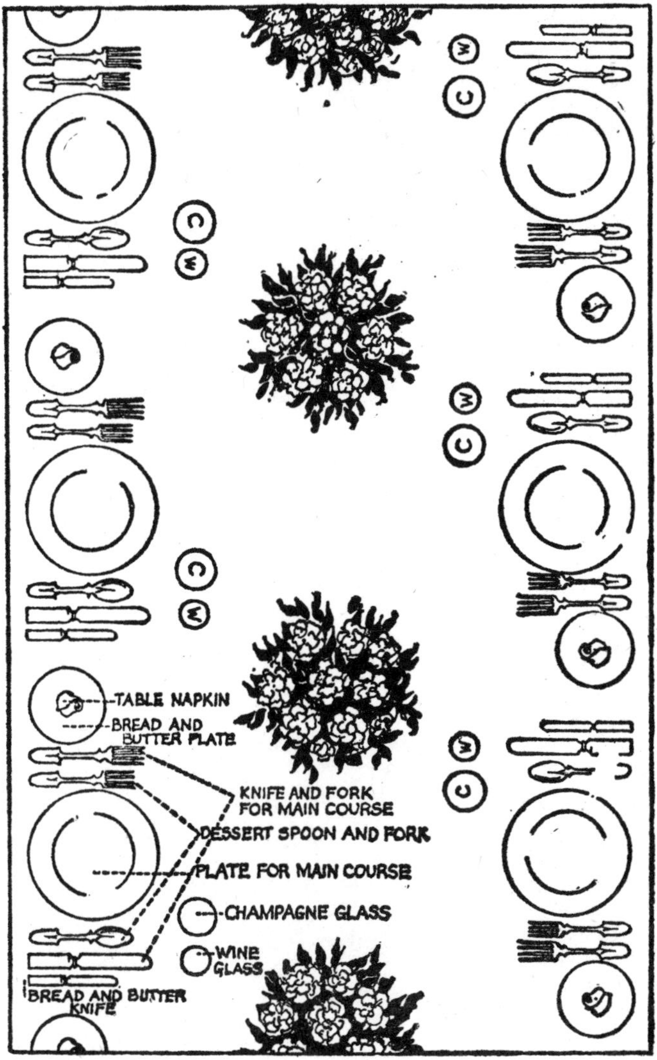

Fig. IV. Suggested setting of section of table for a simple wedding breakfast, consisting of a main meat course, cold with salad, desert, wine and champagne.